D0489703

Knowledg
in the Dig

╻ LOAN

For my wife Deirdre,
with love and admiration

# Knowledge Management in the Digital Newsroom

Stephen Quinn

**Focal Press**

AMSTERDAM BOSTON HEIDELBERG LONDON NEW YORK OXFORD
PARIS SAN DIEGO SAN FRANCISCO SINGAPORE SYDNEY TOKYO

Focal Press
An imprint of Elsevier Science
Linacre House, Jordan Hill, Oxford OX2 8DP
200 Wheeler Road, Burlington, MA 01803

First published 2002
Reprinted 2003

**British Library Cataloguing in Publication Data**
Quinn, Stephen
    Knowledge management in the digital newsroom
    1. Knowledge management   2. News agencies
    I. Title
    070.4´3

**Library of Congress Cataloging in Publication Data**
A catalogue record for this book is available from the Library of
Congress

ISBN 0 240 51677 X

For information on all Focal Press publications
visit our web site at www.focalpress.com

Printed and bound in Great Britain by Biddles Ltd
*www.biddles.co.uk*

# Contents

# Foreword

The Google Web page says it all: 'search 1.6 billion Web pages'. And that's just one search engine. Multiply those pages by the number of available search engines and other means of accessing online information and the problem is stark for digital age journalists. Billions of pages available at the click of a mouse. All to be harnessed, managed, checked, refined.

The difficulty with journalism in the digital age is quite simple: technology allows information overload. We sink beneath its relentless search. Journalists must, to survive, learn quickly and become totally at home with the new technology that is now a staple part of every newsroom, however small or large; whether print, broadcast or online. Technology is what they live by. The difficulty is that unless great care is taken, technology can become the be all and end all of journalistic endeavour and output; technology must never become the message; merely the means of communicating the message more simply, more quickly, more accurately and with better and more interesting facts.

Technology is not the controller; the journalist remains in control. But to exercise that control the journalist now has to be completely at ease with information systems, information management and the changing ways of accessing and developing the raw data and information that one stroke of a computer key can provide from any search engine. The develop-

ment of information management and the need for all journalists to be digitally literate also mean that enormous efforts
must be put into checking and cross-checking to ensure that
the sources being culled from digital or Internet sources are
indeed what they seem. This in turn means that the journalist today has to cope with an enormous amount of information overload. And this too needs managing, both individually and editorially. And the managers and editors themselves,
even though possibly of a different generation to the reporters
and journalists doing the day-to-day work in a newsroom,
must also be digitally literate, not scared of the new technology, and able to harness it for the good of journalism.
Journalists use technology to provide better, faster, more
accurate journalism. The technology must never use journalists for its own end.

Such change in newsrooms, newsroom working and the way
information is accessed requires leadership from the top. And
that means that not just the reporters have to be well trained
and knowledgeable about these new ways of working. The
editors and older generation in every newsroom also need the
same ability. There are editors and managers in almost every
newsroom who are scared of what technology has unleashed.
They can use Quark (just about) and the computer as a word
processor. To them it is little more than an upgraded typewriter. They remain digitally illiterate (or at least not confi-
dently literate) and so cannot achieve the full potential that
proper leadership can achieve in the digital newsroom of the
present and future. So the digital approach to journalism and
information retrieval and management means retraining as
well as training. Journalism education now needs to target
existing as well as new members of the profession. Only then
will information be found, processed and communicated in
the best possible ways for the readers and listeners and viewers (university journalism schools take note!).

The importance – and vastness and dangers – of the new
information management systems was brought home to me

when I read (on the Internet, where else?) that in June 2001 in China alone there were more than 26 million Internet users. The Chinese media report put the increase in China's Internet usage at about 8 million a year. But then I double checked (a lesson to be learnt from the early days of information management in this new digital age). Others, such as the Freedom Forum, believe the numbers are much larger because so many who use the Internet are unregistered, a fact not mentioned in the Chinese media reports. The Freedom Forum believes from their research that the ratio of unregistered to registered users is 4:1, giving a total of well over 100 million users in this one country. In any case, the potential for information retrieval from such countries is enormous.

Internet bars have mushroomed in China since they first appeared in 1997. They've quickly spread to bookstores, barbershops, clothes stores – even the butchers. They have made cyberspace almost impossible to regulate. And of course, in the fast-changing world of journalism, every one of these bars and Internet cafés can be, with no difficulty at all, a mini newsroom, collecting and disseminating information to be sent to other users; to central newsrooms or direct into the online newspaper system. Well, at least they could, until 21 July 2001 when, according to a Reuters report (again seen on the Internet) the Chinese authorities closed down nearly 2000 Internet cafés across the country and ordered 6000 more to suspend operations and make changes.

Thus is the power of the Internet and the need for digital literacy daily becoming more evident. Journalists now only have to type one word into their search engine and many thousands of options immediately appear for them to choose to research. This in itself means a whole new ball game for journalism research. And information management both individually and in newsrooms for all journalists is therefore not only changing but essential for the twenty-first-century journalist and broadcaster. It means every journalist has now to be digitally literate; has to be trained in the complexities of the digital future; has to be able to research quickly, and accurately, with sufficient cross-checking to ensure accuracy. The name of the journalistic game is, without doubt, change. Times they are achangin' for all journalists, of whatever age, of whatever experience. This in turn means that journalism itself is changing with convergence, with the rapid growth of information systems and therefore management. And this in turn means that journalists themselves have to change. It could even mean that the days of the solo-flyer; the rugged individual who searches out his story through good foot leather or through contacts in the pub or through the daily calls to newsmakers and news-making organizations such as the police, fire brigade, ambulance and so on, is rapidly becoming a dinosaur of the twentieth-century age. Sad it may be, but inevitable it certainly is.

The modern journalist must be, and therefore must be trained to be, a team worker, able to use and make use of the information gained by others as part of the team. Newsrooms are changing as the computerized society that is emerging changes attitudes to work, approaches to work, ideas of where stories come from and even what makes news. The proximity viewpoint that has long been one of the stock-in-trade definitions of news editors the world over (1 dead here equals 50 dead somewhere else; and 100 dead somewhere even further away) is itself being rewritten and rethought because proximity, with online and convergent media communication, is now fast becoming everywhere. Information management has to cope with this and find the necessary solutions. Likewise it has to cope with the changes that it will itself provoke in newsrooms, newsroom management, newsroom working and in the mindset of the journalists of the future.

And in a nutshell, that's why this book is so important because it addresses these and other weighty problems associated with the development of information management in the journalistic world. This book opens for us all the future of journalism and the ways in which the problems that the future unfolds can be addressed and solved. It is a book for all of us – editors, reporters, subeditors, broadcasters, online workers – as we embark on the unknown of the digital age journalism.

This is a book of its time. And it has arrived just in time.

John Herbert
Professor of Journalism, Staffordshire University, UK

# Introduction

Information has traditionally been the lifeblood of any newsroom. At the micro level of reporting, information is the reporter's raw material. At the macro level of newsroom management, editors will increasingly need to know how to manage information as well as people. This book looks at the information management tools and processes that have become available to help journalists and media executives deal with information. It attempts to answer some of the pressing issues that news organizations face as they move from operating in the industrial age to succeeding in the information or knowledge age. Along the way, this book considers the possibilities for better journalism and better editorial management.

## Outline of the book

Chapter 1 defines knowledge management and its relationship to information and data, in the context of an environment of information overload. It investigates the factors that are driving change in the media world in the early twenty-first century. News organizations must change to accommodate their customers. People expect news to be available when they want it, in a form that suits their needs. And if content is indeed a news organization's most valuable asset, then this content must be nurtured. This process requires new skills and approaches for a new knowledge-based age.

Chapter 2 outlines what needs to happen for knowledge management to flourish in the newsroom. It calls for changes to the editorial mindset and the way that journalists perceive their role. It suggests that the physical shape of the newsroom must alter, and that journalists must re-define their attitudes to technology. Committed leadership is needed to foster an environment that encourages learning and facilitates change.

Chapter 3 traces the evolution of multiple or convergence journalism in several parts of the world and sees it as an example of the early evolution to the knowledge-based newsroom. It looks at how news organizations around the world are re-organizing their newsrooms to deal with information in new ways. It also considers the tensions apparent in the opposing desires to cut costs and yet maintain journalistic quality.

Chapter 4 introduces the notion of sharing knowledge through intranets. It develops the idea of collaboration introduced in chapter 2. It also offers ways to use intranets and related technology to do better journalism.

Chapter 5 looks at the tools available to information-age journalists. It describes refined forms of information management such as computer-assisted reporting and geographical information systems, and looks at technologies that can help news-gathering. It also introduces extensible markup language or XML, the building block of convergence.

Chapter 6 discusses tools to help reporters become more mobile. It looks at ways in which technology permits the development of the virtual newsroom and outlines the issues that need to be considered in the move to more mobile reporting. Again, leadership is needed to ensure that journalists are not stuck in an office reporting via the telephone and the Internet.

Chapter 7 considers ways to evolve the newsroom to a point where knowledge management can flourish. It looks at how journalism is changing in the context of the accelerated news reporting cycle and revisits the need for a stronger ethical foundation. This chapter also suggests the new role university journalism programmes could be playing in preparing graduates. It works from the basis that journalists need to prepare themselves to become life-long learners.

A section entitled 'How to learn more' is provided at the end of each chapter to help journalists and editorial mangers find resources for dealing with issues raised. Each chapter also includes a list of recommended readings.

# Acknowledgements

Many people helped with the research for this book. It is impossible to name everyone but I would like to express my thanks to several people. Kerry Northrup of Ifra proved a wonderful source of information. He knows more about knowledge management as it applies to journalism than anyone I've met. Many editorial managers gave me their valuable time. In particular I would like to thank Paul Cheung, Chief Editor of Ming Pao Newspapers in Hong Kong; John Beeston and Alan Morison of CNN Asia–Pacific, also in Hong Kong; Mark Bruer of News International in Sydney; Colin McKinnon of *The Age* in Melbourne; George Brock of *The Times* in London; Gil Thelen of the *Tampa Tribune*; Steve Doyle of the *Orlando Sentinel*; Maureen Goggin and Eric Bauer of the *Boston Globe*; Tom Johnson of Boston University; Dr Klaus Viedebantt of the *Frankfurter Allgemeine Zeitung*; Dean Roper and Brian Veseling of Ifra in Darmstadt; Frank Kelett of the Pacific Area Newspaper Publishers' Association; and Debbie Wolfe of the *St Petersburg Times*. Finally, this book would never have been written without the support of my family. My thanks and love go to my wife, Deirdre Quinn-Allan, and our children Tobi and Felix for their patience and tolerance for all those times I came home grumpy and tired.

Stephen Quinn

# About the author

Stephen Quinn joined Zayed University in the United Arab Emirates as an associate professor of journalism in August 2001. He was previously a senior lecturer in journalism at Deakin University in Victoria, Australia. He started as a cadet reporter on the *Newcastle Morning Herald* in Australia in 1975. While there he was introduced to sub-editing because it was company policy that all cadets spent time on the subs' table. He later worked as a reporter on the *Central Coast Express* at Gosford and the *Singleton Argus*, both in New South Wales in Australia. At the *Argus* he was the sole journalist, which meant he had to report and sub his own copy and write all headlines for three editions a week. He moved to Sydney on completing his BA in 1977 and worked as a sub-editor with *The Australian Women's Weekly*, then Australia's premier magazine.

In March 1979 he travelled overland to England. Between June 1979 and the end of 1982 he was a sub-editor with the Press Association in Fleet Street and BBC-TV's teletext service Ceefax in west London. In 1983 he was appointed the founding editor and manager of Television New Zealand's teletext service, Teletext. He returned to London in 1986, where he was a writer and sub-editor with Independent Television News (ITN) from 1986 to 1988, and a public relations consultant and later national public relations manager for the UK subsidiary of Wang in 1988–1989. Stephen joined *The Guardian* in London in 1989 as a sub-editor on the arts desk.

The next year he moved to New Zealand, where he ran two journalism programmes between 1991 and 1995. During that time he maintained his involvement with journalism via training courses and freelance writing. He returned to Australia in 1996 to take up a university teaching position. He received his PhD in 1999. Dr Quinn has maintained close links with industry by contributing to newspapers and magazines, working as a casual sub-editor and running training courses. He is married with three children, aged 20, 12 and 7.

Dr Quinn is the author of *Digital Sub-editing and Design* (Focal Press, 2001); *Newsgathering on the Net*, second edition (Macmillan, 2001); and *The Art of Learning* (Deakin University Press, 1999).

# 1

# Knowledge management and journalism

## Executive summary

This book proceeds from the idea that journalists and editorial executives need to work smarter in the information age. Productivity and success will come more from intangibles such as knowledge management rather than from doing the same things over and over again, such as looking for more ways to cut costs. Knowledge management is one of the key tools of the information age. This chapter looks first at the big picture, presenting the drivers that are producing massive change all over the world. It then defines knowledge in relation to the tools journalists have previously used – data and information. And then it considers the possible scenarios that will lead to change in the newsroom. All of this is coming about because consumers expect news to be available in a variety of forms to suit their lifestyles. News organizations must consequently learn to accommodate their customers. In this book, each summary lists the sections of that chapter in the order they are covered so that busy people can go directly to the relevant section. Topics covered in this chapter include:

- ❏ information a glut product
- ❏ from information scarcity to surplus
- ❏ declines in circulation
- ❏ technology a powerful driver
- ❏ social and economic causes of change
- ❏ the role of media giants
- ❏ changes in consumer attitudes

❑ managing knowledge in the newsroom
❑ new skills for the knowledge age
❑ new approaches for a new age.

Data and information are the raw materials of journalism. Good journalism attracts audiences and advertisers to all forms of the commercial media. It is also the reason people listen to public service broadcasters. So the ability to produce good journalism – itself the result of high quality newsgathering – should be one of the major activities of news organizations. But, in the new millennium, content based on simple data and information will not be enough. As the information age evolves, journalists and editorial executives will also need to work with knowledge. From the start we should distinguish these three things in the context of journalism. So let's begin with a few definitions. Data are raw, undifferentiated facts. We could liken data to apples on a tree: until the apples are harvested or processed, only a few people have access to them and those apples have relatively low value. Read or placed out of context, facts often have no connection or link with other facts. But apples can be picked and boxed for sale or export. The people who pick and process the apples make them more manageable, more accessible. They also make the apples available for further adaptation or processing – apple pies or toffee apples, perhaps – and the apples consequently acquire more value.

Similarly, information is data that has been processed, refined and placed in context. The root of the word comes from the Latin *informare*, to give shape to, or fashion. The *Concise Oxford Dictionary* defines information as news or 'the act of telling or informing'. It has the related connotation of teaching and imparting knowledge. People who possess information are said to be 'informed'. Leading journalism thinker Professor Tom Johnson of Boston University believes that in the opening years of the twenty-first century journalists, journalism educators and scholars must recognize that huge amounts of data of all sorts exist somewhere in the world in digital form. He builds on the seminal insight of information theorists Shannon and Weaver (1963) who pointed out that data are the raw material of analysis. 'Information is that which reduces uncertainty and, therefore, assists in making a decision or reaching a conclusion about a question or issue' (Johnson, 2001: 4).

Knowledge is the result of further refining of information and further placing in context, into a form that readers and viewers find even more useful or that saves them time and money. Knowledge management consultant Alan Burton-Jones rejects the traditional economic view that information and knowledge are the same. He defines knowledge as the 'cumulative stock of information and skills derived from the *use* of information' (my italics). The value and meaning we ascribe to knowledge increases in relation to the thinking and acting involved to create it and place it in context (Burton-Jones, 1999: 5–6). This book proceeds from a simple premise: knowledge management is important for media groups because they must become information-based organizations to compete in the information age. Knowledge management enhances journalists' use of data and information, their raw material. It is about improving professional practice and helping journalists learn how to do better journalism. It involves learning how to store, transfer and share information in a form that makes it useful both now and in the future. It involves a new professional culture that fosters teamwork and collaboration. And it involves learning how to manage information systematically, rather than the chaotic approach that too many journalists have used in the past. Knowledge management began primarily as a business tool, but it should not be dismissed as merely a business process. Media organizations are businesses and journalists could learn much from what business has gained in terms of data management and the knowledge economy. Indeed, journalists need to be willing to learn from the professional practices of many different groups, among them information scientists, librarians and data architects.

## Information a glut product

Knowledge management guru Karl-Erik Sveiby points out that mass media markets teach people that information is a glut product. Indeed, media companies seem increasingly happy to give it away. Witness the flood of free daily newspapers and weekly magazines in cities as far afield as Boston, Melbourne, London, Singapore and the Scandinavian countries, and with more planned in other parts of the world. Sveiby also notes that information requires readers and listeners to work – they have to convert it into something useful (1996: 386). Journalists have traditionally changed data into information during the newsgathering process. Some of the key roles of journalism in the information age will be to turn information into knowledge – to make it *more useful* for their audiences – and to find ways to preserve knowledge for later adaptation. This takes training and skill, both of which require investments of time and money. As Sveiby notes, 'it

**Figure 1.1** The control room of the converged newsroom at CNN Asia–Pacific's headquarters in Hong Kong. Photograph Stephen Quinn

takes knowledge and energy to convert passive information into something that can be acted upon' (1996: 386). Academics have given the new era we live in various names, including the 'information age', the 'third industrial revolution' and the 'post-industrial age'. Information-rich nations tend to be rich in other ways. The more complex a society, the more it needs information and knowledge workers. The boom in the US economy in the last decade of the twentieth century came about because its infrastructure, laws and government encouraged the availability and free flow of information. During the Cold War from the 1940s until the 1980s the American government funded the vast bulk (85 per cent) of the country's research and development. Information tends to increase with the invention and introduction of new knowledge-handling technology. Groups of knowledge workers arise, who in turn increase the amount of information for that group, especially as their work gets more complex (Cortada, 1998: 10). Certainly that has been the case in the past. The telegraph forced journalists to boost their skills and education levels radically in the middle of the nineteenth century, otherwise they could not compete. Similarly, journalists needed to acquire other talents such as learning Pitman shorthand and typing to make themselves employable (Standage, 1998: 69–70). The same need for training and learning arises in the information age.

The information age will require better-educated journalists and need organizations that invest in their staff. News organizations will need both to be able to evolve and survive. Put simply, knowledge management concerns the organization of a company's non-tangible assets. Given the primacy of information and knowledge in the information age, editorial staff need to understand and apply the principles of knowledge management to their job. This chapter describes the concept of information and knowledge and applies it to journalism, in the context of a changing profession and a changing world. Several factors are driving change in the modern world of journalism. In no specific order of importance these drivers include an oversupply of data, declining weekday circulations at newspapers, declining audiences for free-to-air television, and major social and economic disruptions. Rapid developments in technology are also producing major upheavals. All of these mean major changes to the ways that consumers want to receive their news. These drivers have already changed, and will continue to transform, the journalism environment in coming years. It's useful to begin by discussing them.

## From information scarcity to surplus

The first driver for change is information overload. It is referred to in various other terms such as data smog, information anxiety and data excess. But the problem remains the same – overwhelming amounts of data distort our attempts to make valid decisions quickly. Steve Yelvington, a news consultant, believes the challenge for media companies is to understand this radical shift from information scarcity to surplus. This means a new role for journalists as guide rather than gatekeeper, he says, and the need for new ways of running news businesses that will support the journalist's new role. Yelvington noted that this was 'infinitely harder than keeping up with technological changes' (quoted in Outing, 2000). *The Economist* magazine reported that in the late 1990s mankind produced about a million books a year, each with an average 300 pages. Americans sent about 610 billion emails in 2000. The magazine estimated that the world produced about two exabytes of information that year (an exabyte is roughly a billion times a billion bytes), and predicted that the production of data would continue to increase. IBM consultant James Cortada noted that humans have always tried to augment human knowledge and develop ways to store it. People then look for standards, as a way to improve that information capture. 'We see [the] need for information followed by standards and conventions to ensure effective use of the tools' (Cortada, 1998: 6). Thus the Egyptians invented papyrus and the Chinese paper 'to augment human memory'. After that came books, moveable type, adding machines, typewriters, calculators and finally the computer. The volume of information grew. The great Library of Alexandria that Ptolemy I established in 290 BC reportedly held 700 000 volumes. By the start of the sixteenth century in Europe there were between 15 and 20 million books. In 1998 the USA alone published 40 000 books a year. In the half century to the year 2000, the world spent more than US$4 000 000 million on computers (Cortada, 1998: 7). The Hudson Institute (http://www.hudson.org), an international public policy institute based in Minneapolis in Minnesota that forecasts trends and developments, summarized the complexity of twenty-first century life: 'In one year people now have to absorb an amount of information that took [them] 100 years to absorb 400 years ago'. Huge improvements in technology are driving much of this excess, creating the need to manage change.

Sveiby says an excess of supply over demand characterizes all modern information markets. 'Information is becoming ever easier to produce, whereas human capacity to absorb information is changing only slowly. The capacity cannot be enhanced to any significant degree, except by higher education' (1996: 386). Burton-Jones believes that society is drowning in information 'but still left thirsty for knowledge' (1999: 219). In the twenty-first century, information comes quickly but truth takes time, writes Jon Katz. A generation ago, the death of Diana, Princess of Wales, would have been a two-day wonder. But powerful technologies such as satellite, 24-hour cable and the Web morphed her demise into a global story. 'As more Americans wire up to the Internet, the traditional role of the reporter – the one who tells you what is happening – is being radically transformed and supplanted.' As the Starr Report showed, says Katz, Americans increasingly can get the news before journalists do (2000: 44–45). New technologies make the idea of trained, ethical fact-gatherers and truthtellers 'more essential than ever' (Katz, 2000: 50). Journalist David Shenk, author of *Data Smog*, similarly concluded that journalists were more necessary than ever in the information-glutted world. 'As a skeptical analytical buffer and – now more than ever – as an arbiter of statistical claims, the news media is an indispensable public utility, every bit as vital as our electricity and gas lines. In a world with vastly more information than it can process, journalists are the most important processors we have' (Shenk, 1997: 166–67). The director general of the World Association of Newspapers, Timothy Balding, told the association's 2001 annual conference in Hong Kong that information overload was driving specialization at newspapers. Consumers were demanding more relevance and advertisers were demanding better targeting. Communities of interest were moving from a localized geographic base to a situation where people formed groups based on interest but the members were spread around the world (Balding, 2001).

## Declines in circulation

Circulation in mature markets was declining and newspapers were competing more and more for readers' time, Balding said. Figures from the Newspaper Association of America (http://www.naa.org) showed that daily newspaper circulation (morning and evening) rose slightly from 53.8 million in 1950 to 56.9 million in 1996. But the population grew from about 151 million to about 270 million during the same period. Data from the Canadian Newspaper Association (http://www.cna-acj.ca) showed that total newspaper circulation dropped from 5.4 million in 1980 to 5.1 million in 1999. Again, this decline came about despite an increasing population. The average number of newspapers that American households bought each day dropped from just over 1.1 in 1960 to 0.5 forty years later (Kees, 2000: 2–3). In Australia, the combined circulation of all dailies Monday to Friday declined just over 10 per cent in the decade to March 2001. Saturday circulation for the same period rose slightly, by 0.6 per cent. Combined, the overall circulation dropped by 4.7 per cent. The Australian data were only available for a decade because the country's publishers had long resisted pressures to present data separately for Monday to Friday and Saturday figures (Pacific Area Newspaper Publishers' Association (PANPA) *Bulletin* May 2001: 10). During that decade, the country's population rose 11.5 per cent from 17.3 million to 19.3 million (Australian Bureau of Statistics, 2001). Healthy economies in some countries in the last three years of the twentieth century balanced the falls in circulation. A booming economy has meant that advertising incomes, in constant terms, were better than the highest levels of the 1980s boom in Europe, North America and the Asia–Pacific region. PANPA reported in the July 2000 edition of its *Bulletin* that, on a global level, advertising incomes were up 18.8 per cent in 1999 compared with 1987.

The 53rd annual conference of the World Association of Newspapers held in Rio de Janeiro, Brazil in June 2000 noted that circulation losses in the European Union were only 0.1 per cent in 1999. This was only one-fifth of the loss in 1998 and one-tenth of the 1997 loss. Newspaper readership actually increased in western Europe in 1999, by just over 1 per cent to 62.1 per cent of all adults. The Japanese newspaper market remained 'resilient', the *Bulletin* reported, with a 0.2 per cent increase between 1994 and 1999. Japan retained its position as the world leader in the number of daily sales – 72 218 000. India saw sales decline by 3.6 per cent in 1999 after five years of growth but still sat in second place in the total number of sales – 60 million in 1999. The USA was in third place with 56 million and China fourth, with 50 million daily sales (PANPA *Bulletin*, 2000: 14–15). The World Association of Newspaper's next yearly survey, released at its annual conference in Hong Kong in June 2001, noted that newspaper readership in Western Europe increased in 2000 by more than 1 per cent, and 62.1 per cent of all European adults still read a daily newspaper. But the population increased by more than 1 per cent. Daily circulation figures rose in eight of the fifteen European Union countries in 2000 but declined in the rest. Over the five years to 2000, newspaper sales in the fifteen European Union countries fell 2.5 per cent – a loss of 2.06 million newspaper buyers. Over the decade to 2000, the drop in circulation amounted to 3.4 per cent, or 2.9 million fewer newspaper buyers. The Japanese market saw a slight dip of 0.4 per cent in 2000 and a total decline of 1.1 per cent in the previous five years, a good achievement given the country was in recession. Papers in the USA experienced a slight decline of 1.1 per cent but, over the decade to 2000, the total fall was 10.2 per cent, meaning that 6.38 million fewer people were buying a paper in 2000 compared with 1990. India continued to stride forward with increased sales of 20.2 per cent in 2000. Over the decade, sales had risen 28.7 per cent. When comparing total circulation, Japan remained in front with 71 896 000 copies sold daily. India was next with 66 million; the USA third with 55 943 000 followed by China (50 million) and Germany with 23 946 000 (Balding, 2001). With more and more niche markets emerging, we can expect changes in newspapers in the form we currently know them. The question is how will they change?

**Figure 1.2** This mural at Ifra's headquarters in Darmstadt in Germany combines the flag or nameplate of thousands of Ifra member publications. Photograph Stephen Quinn

## Technology a powerful driver

Technology is another driver. Some analysts suggest it is the most powerful. It has changed journalism radically in the past two decades and will continue to transform it further. Jon Katz believes that publishers and editorial executives have never known how to respond to technology, or the culture it spawns and transmits. 'They dismissed rock and roll as an obnoxious craze, relegated movies to the back of the book and ridiculed TV as frivolous entertainment ... The Internet was portrayed as a den of hackers, perverts, pornographers, cyber-addicts and thieves. Each time, journalism seems caught short, reacting rather than initiating, backing up, catching up.' At the same time, technology has overwhelmed media, 'devouring it, stealing its customers, transforming its values, changing its role and its relationship to the public, usurping its long, sometimes even honored role, as keeper of our [American] national civic agenda' (Katz, 2000: 44).

Approaches to dealing with the impact of technology vary, but forward-looking editorial managers appreciate that things have to change. The executive editor of the *News & Observer* in Raleigh, North Carolina, Anders Gyllenhaal, in an address to the Association for Education in Journalism and Mass Communication, concluded that technology 'needs to play a much bigger role than ever before' at newspapers (2000: 16). 'Why is it so hard for newsrooms to use technology well?' he asked. 'We write and talk about it all the time. Why don't we do more to follow our own advice?' (2000: 18). Journalism educator Bruce Garrison is disappointed at the way that jour-nalists have reacted to technology. 'It seems like we don't know what the missed opportunities are. I'm not sure we even know what we could be doing in terms of newsgather-ing' (quoted in Boyer, 1999: 48). Stephen Miller, assistant to the technology editor at *The New York Times*, points out that journalism is a different profession today. 'The major change is where information resides and how journalists get to it.' He believes that most reporters and editors are 'behind the curve' in using technology for better journalism. Journalists are simply not efficient in the way they gather and analyse news. 'One of the reasons is lack of knowledge and training. Training is not a priority in most [US] newsrooms' (Miller, 1999: 34). George Landau, whose company 'NewsEngin' develops knowledge management tools tailored for the news-room, agrees with Miller and Garrison. 'I think journalists tend not to be plugged in as well as the rest of the world in terms of what's possible for technology.' Landau has opted for a two-pronged attack on information overload. He developed software that made it easier to share relational database infor-mation (this consists of the highly structured data about things and people that newsrooms hold). Landau has made it easier for journalists to gather, organize, search and share the looser kinds of data that journalists encounter – interview notes, email, wire stories and source documents. 'I was cer-tain that one day in the not-so-distant future, all newsrooms would be equipped with something similar to the tools that I envisioned' (Landau, 1999: 29–30). Landau's company (http://www.newsengin.com) offers two free tools from the home page – a cost-of-living calculator and a percentage change calculator.

This book will argue that technology should not control choice. Rather, it provides options for people who make deci-sions. It is a tool to be used to do better journalism. But tech-nology is a powerful driver. It is one of the reasons we have so much more data – via the Web, satellites, mobile phones, email and other communications technology. These provide more and more opportunities to generate more and more information. Because this book concerns itself with technolo-gy, various potential scenarios and solutions are discussed in later chapters. Technology is also changing employment roles, in the sense that in the high-tech automated world of the 1990s a new elite of knowledge workers emerged with critical skills that elevated them to centre stage in the global economy. Economist Jeremy Rifkin maintains they are fast becoming 'the new aristocracy' (2000: 175). In the 1970s, the sort of work that went offshore from industrialized nations consisted of low-tech, low productivity jobs such as making toys and clothing. But by the 1990s, because of computers, advanced telecommunications and cheap transport, high-tech jobs started moving to developing countries with cheaper labour. Witness the rise of southern India's version of Silicon Valley in Bangalore, where companies such as IBM, Hewlett-Packard, Motorola and Texas Instruments set up shop to take advantage of the country's scientists and engineers. Global companies in the USA and Japan have been setting up production plants along the 500-km border between Mexico and the USA since the late 1970s (Rifkin, 2000: 204). Rifkin lists journalists among the new elite of knowledge workers, though membership depends on their knowledge of technology.

## Social and economic causes of change

Consultant Katherine Fulton maintains that social and economic drivers are more powerful than technology, though she concedes that the Internet is a catalyst for change. 'The main event isn't technology,' she says, 'it's economic and social change. The Internet is not just another media delivery system, like television and radio before it. It's the catalyst for a historic transition from one era to another'. She is talking about the information age, where the ability to assemble and transform information into knowledge will be more important than mere industrial-age skills. 'Basic headline news, provided by many players, has become ubiquitous, a commodity, because the Internet has trained people to expect free information.' Meanwhile, competition from new players will increase. Traditional media will be able to distinguish themselves through good reporting, but it is expensive. 'Good multi-media reporting, distributed in many different ways for many different purposes, will be even more expensive.' Fulton believes that only healthy businesses will be able to pay for it. 'That means two types of winners: small and very focused, or large. Medium-sized players need not apply' (Fulton, 2000: 30). Fulton concludes that consolidation among general-interest local news players is inevitable and, if that happens, the likely winners are strong local media who form partnerships. The good news is that journalism and journalists 'could become more essential than ever'. Smart journalists will embrace new forms of journalism such as multi-media storytelling and learn to take advantage of archival resources 'aggregating and repackaging reporting from many sources'. Wise journalists will find ways to employ their traditional abilities to synthesize, explain and place events in context. 'They'll also work to re-interpret those old values for a new era.' The difficult part, she concedes, is 'knowing what to hold onto and what to let go [of]' (Fulton, 2000: 35).

## The role of media giants

The media market place has also changed. A quarter of a century ago, media companies played a relatively insignificant role in the economy compared with the then dominant players in manufacturing, mining, oil and production. But the rise of media giants has illustrated the power of information and knowledge as commodities. American academic Robert McChesney has predicted that in time, five to eight huge companies will dominate the US market, and 50 to 80 companies will control the world information market. The eight world giants – AOL Time Warner, News Corporation, Disney, Viacom, General Electric, Vivendi-Universal, Sony Corporation and Bertelsmann – generated revenues of US$358 700 million in calendar year 2000 – significantly more than the GDP of many countries (McChesney, 1999: 86–88). Despite the concentration of ownership – and the potential dangers for democracy – consumers faced significantly more choice at the start of the third millennium. Jon Katz believes that the giant corporations taking over media companies 'love technology' because 'it helps them reach many millions of customers, makes much more money. As media become more corporatized, their greedy and soulless new owners use technology to mass-market information, transforming much of journalism into just another form of entertainment' (Katz, 2000: 44). We are witnessing a huge increase in the volume of media available to consumers, and a shrinking of the number of companies that provide content. Former media competitors are joining forces. Bob Ingle, president of Knight Ridder Ventures, noted that American media companies were looking for ways to expand beyond their editorial content. 'We always believed the editorial content was the crown jewel, but we've found it's not enough. We are having to put services and features into [our] Web sites, and the e-commerce stuff, and online shopping sites. Editorial content will draw them there. But so will a lot of free services' (quoted in Shepard, 2000: 26). Tom Brew, a former editor of MSNBC.com, agreed: 'You think editorial is what drives this world? No. It's money. It's about advertising' (quoted in Shepard, 2000: 26). Terence Smith, media reporter for the PBS *News Hour with Jim Lehrer* believes television news executives are 'genuinely concerned about the worst trends toward tabloidization – the blurring between entertainment and the news – and the lowering of standards'. He said the key problem was the fact that the three biggest television networks in the USA were part of larger corporations and those networks 'don't spend a lot of time worrying about journalistic standards'. Consequently, news executives had 'lost their voice or place at the table in a much more corporate work environment' (Smith, 2001: 4D).

## Changes in consumer attitudes

Ifra's managing director, Gunther Bottcher, noted in *Ifra Trends 2001* that the future would be a buyers' market. 'Consumers will have an almost unlimited set of products to choose from, and they will choose the products that match their interests and that are of superior quality. Quality of content will be the most important success factor, but quality of production, packaging and display should not be undervalued.' Bottcher cited optimal use of technology, flexibility, speed and modern organization and management systems as strategic factors to ensure success, combined with teamwork.

'All members of an organization must develop digital, data-centric and marketing-oriented thinking' (Bottcher, quoted in *Ifra Trends* 2001: 4). This was because the successful news organization would focus on information rather than production. Content remains important. What you do with it is equally vital. Some news organizations are looking at other forms of delivery of content such as mobile data. This is discussed in chapter 6. Arthur Sulzberger Jr, Publisher of *The New York Times*, summarized some publishers' thinking when he said: 'I'm not in the newspaper business ... Right now, many of our people want it on paper and we will try to serve that market. ... If they want it beamed directly into their minds, we will create a cerebral cortex edition'. In September 2000, New York Times Digital, the Internet division of The New York Times Company, launched a global, around-the-clock news, information and entertainment service built on the wireless application protocol (WAP). The service, called NYT Mobile, offers updates from NYTimes.com's top stories, as well as the latest international, political, technology, finance and sports news. NYT Mobile's content is also available for short messaging service (SMS) delivery as well. WAP and SMS technology will allow New York Times Digital to develop more applications for delivery to the screens of mobile devices. Content from New York Times Digital is available on other wireless devices, including pagers and PDAs (personal digital appliances). The company has also made the newspaper available in many parts of the USA via digital distribution. Using NewsStand technology, subscribers get access to the newspaper via the Internet. The online version has the same design, words and advertisements as the print edition.

The New York Times Company took a minority equity position in NewsStand (http://www.newsstand.com) based in Austin in Texas. In June 2001, NewsStand opened offices in Japan, England (Newcastle), Australia (Sydney) and Germany (Munich) to expand its digital circulation service. The New York Times Company is an example of how organizations are making information available in a multitude of forms.

This 're-purposing' of content is already happening in several countries, and is one of the most likely developments as the century evolves. It is discussed in chapter 3.

## Managing knowledge in the newsroom

Fulton and others acknowledge that information and the knowledge created with it remain the lifeblood of news organizations. What journalists gather, share, store and publish therefore becomes a news organization's most valuable asset, though one must concede that advertising is also vital. For Dean Roper, editor of Ifra's monthly journal, *newspaper techniques*, the big question is how are newsrooms managing this information and knowledge? 'Most in the industry say that newsrooms are changing but that the majority of newsrooms are falling far too short; editors and reporters say that the ability to manage this knowledge which will be published, republished, re-purposed is becoming greatly enhanced, yet it's still a struggle at best.'

Ifra (http://www.ifra.com) represents more than 1800 publishers and technology firms worldwide, and specializes in researching the impact of technology on newspapers. Roper believes that if newspapers are to transform themselves into knowledge management companies, it is up to editors, reporters and editorial managers to 'lead this crusade'. Dr Dae-Whan Chang, the publisher of South Korea's business daily the *Maeil Business Newspaper*, aims to make his publication one of the world's most prestigious 'knowledge newspapers'. He believes knowledge management is the key to the future. 'The new economy has changed the rules of the game. We have new players, new technologies, new paradigms and these require new behaviours. Knowledge is the key word.' He includes a 'knowledge pool' among the key strategies that newspaper companies must adopt for the new millennium (Chang, 2001). Dr Chang is executive chairman of the World Knowledge Forum held each year in Seoul in October. Chapter 7 elaborates on the new strategies needed for the new century and uses *Maeil Business Newspaper* as an example of a transformed news organization.

What is this thing called knowledge management? Sveiby describes it as the art of creating value by leveraging an organization's intangible assets. He maintains that knowledge cannot be managed but prefers the notion of people being 'knowledge focused'. He runs his own consulting company in Australia, 'Sveiby Knowledge Management'. Prior to that he owned a series of Swedish financial magazines. 'You have to be able to visualize your organization as consisting of nothing but knowledge. This is a different mindset from the industrial era paradigm.' The next two chapters consider this cultural shift in the context of the modern newsroom.

For news organizations, their competitive advantage depends on their ability to create and distribute stories that are difficult to imitate. This is probably the simplest application of knowledge management in the context of news organizations. The key is the ability to share information and ideas. Knowledge management involves capturing both explicit intellectual property and human know-how. The latter is sometimes called 'tacit knowledge' – what resides in people's heads. In the digital environment, information can be easily copied and re-processed. The Internet is, after all, the world's biggest photocopying machine. What becomes valuable is what cannot be copied – things like integrity, trust, quality and brand name for an organization, and intellectual firepower and experience for an individual. Journalists create knowledge in the process of synthesizing information, and with time generate reputations for integrity and quality. Successful news organizations will be those that appreciate the importance of good journalism for producing these intangibles. Microsoft boss Bill Gates talks about raising a company's corporate IQ by establishing an atmosphere that promotes knowledge sharing and collaboration. This can be done by prioritizing areas in which knowledge sharing is most valuable, providing the digital tools that make sharing possible and rewarding people 'for contributing to the full flow of information' (1999: 12). Tony Carrozzo, an information systems architect, leads the information systems team at Hewlett-Packard Laboratory's research library in Palo Alto in California. He created Connex, the first knowledge management system used within Hewlett-Packard. He believes the best definition of knowledge management is the ability to locate knowledge when you need it. 'If you can't do that, knowledge may as well not exist.' One of the reasons knowledge management was so important in the new economy, he said, was that technology was ceasing to be a differentiating factor. 'So the only thing that really matters, or is becoming more important, is the intellectual capital that you have.' Rowan Wilson, editor of *Knowledge Management Review*, believes that professional people, including journalists, who fail to take advantage of their knowledge are not working as fast or as smart as they could. 'If you can stop people duplicating the effort, then you're going to be a faster, more responsive work force' (quoted in Lane, 2000).

Knowledge management has existed as a concept, primarily in the business world, for about a decade. Gradually these ideas are entering the newsroom. But they require change: a new culture or mindset, coupled with new tools, new physical environments and a new approach to deadlines. Roper noted that newspapers would seem obvious candidates to adopt this philosophy, given the fact that they deal primarily with information and the creation of knowledge. Some news organizations were beginning to try to adopt the necessary mindset, he said, 'but the industry as a whole is lagging' (2000: 22). Newspapers in particular have traditionally operated as manufacturing industries, as producers of paper products rather than knowledge. That must change. Vince Giuliano, chief executive officer of SimVenture (http://www.simventure.com), maintains that newspapers must transform themselves and see themselves as knowledge companies. 'While the newsroom is at the centre of the newspaper's knowledge capabilities, the newspaper is also a manufacturing company which produces and distributes a new product every day. In terms of costs and economics, a typical newspaper is 30 per cent a knowledge-age organization, and 70 per cent a traditional manufacturing and distribution organization. Therefore, the culture and policies of most newspapers are more like those of traditional manufacturing companies than like those of information-age companies' (personal interviews, Boston, 25 March and 15 April 2001). Giuliano considers the concept of the multiple-journalism newsroom as opening up long-term possibilities for news organizations but believes that changes like these ultimately involve transformation of the journalists' perceptions of their roles and profession. In short, a change of mindset. 'Obtaining the resources to do this requires enrolling the leadership of other departments in the newspaper as well as the top management.' Once those are in place, Giuliano believes there will be an increased willingness to move the newspaper 'towards being a multiple-media organization'. Chapter 3 discusses this form of journalism.

Consultant Andreas Becker suggests that tomorrow's newspaper will be structured to supply information and provide a platform of services that include advertising and business transactions. 'Its business model will encompass all of its services grouped around its core activity of collecting, formatting and analyzing information' (quoted in Arnould, 2000: 45). The executive director of Ifra's Center for Advanced News Operations, Kerry Northrup, says modern newsrooms should be capable of managing very large amounts of raw input data, and be capable of outputting more than just one type of information processed for a single type of media. 'The current wastage between the information a journalist collates and what he/she actually uses for an article in a daily newspaper is enormous.' Ifra writer Valerie Arnould points out that journalists possess large amounts of knowledge that only they know how to use. If they leave a company, this tacit knowledge goes with them (2000: 45).

## New skills for the knowledge age

Northrup believes that the ability to compete in the information economy requires new skills: communicating effectively, working collaboratively, amassing expertise, life-long learning combined with learning from experience and leveraging information assets. 'In the parlance of knowledge management, which is transforming businesses all over the world, it means knowing what you know. And if any organization should be smart when it comes to handling information, it certainly should be a newsroom.' Unfortunately, Northrup says, most newsrooms are not very smart: 'They gather massive volumes of raw news material and then save only the little bit that is published. They employ crowds of trained journalists and then tap only a fraction of their collective news judgment and expertise. They communicate so poorly that it is common to have two desks chasing the same story and not know it' (Northrup, 1999).

A classic example of poor communication occurred at the BBC when news managers discovered that a BBC radio journalist had departed from Heathrow airport on the same flight as a BBC TV journalist – one in business class, the other in economy – to cover the same story. Chris Cramer, president of CNN international networks, told the story in *The Guardian*: 'They stayed in different hotels, covered the story without meeting, and met back at Heathrow as they collected their luggage. This grotesque lack of coordination necessitated change at the BBC, and since then newsgathering staff for radio and TV have operated as one integrated department' (Cramer, 2001). Editorial managers and journalists have agonized over the waste of data every day in news organizations. *The Age* in Melbourne in Australia, which each day produces anywhere from 48 to 120 broadsheet pages for seven days a week, publishes perhaps 1 per cent of all the news data that enter the building. *The New York Times* may have the motto 'All the news that's fit to print' but in reality it's more a case of all the news that fits. Print newspapers are constrained by time and space, and much material that does not fit is wasted. George Landau believes news organizations are 'just plain stupid about managing information'. 'We pay our best journalists handsome salaries to gather the news and then discard 90 per cent of their work product. When we replace one reporter on a beat with another, we often make the new guy start from scratch, with no list of sources, no background, no context. The only scrap of information that stands a chance of being consulted for subsequent stories is the small portion that actually made it into the paper, and hence into the paper's official archive' (quoted in Roper, 2000: 23). Landau said he has come to regard the American newsrooms he sees as funnels. Huge amounts of information pass through them like crude oil sludge: 'A typical newsroom was nothing but an antiquated, inefficient knowledge refinery. Reporters were technologically ill-equipped for the flood of raw material arriving in digital form. Clearly, outfitting those journalists with modern information-management tools had become an urgent necessity for the news industry. Clear to me, anyway' (Landau, 1999: 29).

Newsrooms have traditionally equated their knowledge assets with their digital archives, but have forgotten the huge amount of knowledge in people's heads and contact books. Consultant Gabriella Franzini of EidosMedia in Milan in Italy says digital libraries represent a tiny proportion of the knowledge created by a newsroom. 'While planning a story, journalists gather information from different sources, discuss issues with colleagues, either directly or through email, elaborate and process collected information before finally creating one or more stories. There are cases in which the research work is huge but it may get lost right after since the digital archive will just store published stories. Knowledge systems should allow journalists to access all forms of information so they can work on it collaboratively from any location. All information they obtain should be made available for further uses, to facilitate the creation of more knowledge in an ongoing spiral. Intranet-based technology, as well as collaborative tools and sophisticated search engines, are vital for the deployment of knowledge assets', she says (quoted in Roper, 2000: 25-26). These tools are discussed in chapters 4 and 5.

Franzini maintains that knowledge is a news organization's most important resource. 'Since competition is more and more based on companies' capabilities to empower employees with the information they need to make fast and reliable decisions, it's essential to build a global environment where knowledge creation is treated as a core competence.' She points out that knowledge resides in many different places – databases, filing cabinets, the Internet, intranets, people's heads – and is distributed across different environments. The aim should be to share this explicit and tacit knowledge and make it widely available and channel it into creating innovative products and services. Proper management of intangible knowledge assets allows businesses to generate profits and create customer value, she said. 'It is important to build knowledge on top of information because information by itself does not generate knowledge. Even having information in an appropriate [technical] format does not give knowledge because it is just a way to structure information' (personal interview, Boston, 12 April 2001). In a value system where information is at the centre, technology becomes a key factor and humans are passive processors of it, even when they apply best practices. In a system where knowledge is at the centre, humans are key because they assess the information. 'Technology is just an enabler,' Franzini said. Journalists were engaged in a perpetual processes of learning and unlearning, and technology enabled the implementation of what Franzini called a knowledge newsroom. One key technology was XML, or extensible markup language. 'XML will transform the Internet from a massive collection of unmanageable data into a structured, easily navigable transport for sophisticated business and personal transactions', Franzini said (Franzini, 2001). XML is discussed in chapter 5.

Some journalists simply do not have the skills to deal with

the vast quantity of data they encounter. George Brock, managing editor of *The Times* in London, concedes that reporters have access to huge amounts of data that they sometimes cannot manage. 'Day after day, I watch perfectly competent journalists at *The Times*, some eminent in their fields, wrestle with what most software makers would consider quite 'simple' tasks or simply under-using the system they have. Nobody has yet produced … a knowledge management [system] for writers which allows them to easily manipulate large quantities of electronic data from many different sources' (quoted in Roper, 2000:23). Editorial managers had to create rules and guidelines, Brock said, and often this became an inhibition to creating a 'perfect utopian system of sharing'.

Brock believes newsroom culture is very heavily influenced by the people in charge. 'When I was a foreign correspondent the foreign editor used to ask the foreign correspondents who worked in Europe (of whom I was one) … to write guidance memorandums.' These were circulated to London staff, to correspondents and to the editorial writers. They were known as Reform Club memoranda because the meeting that set up

**Figure 1.3** The expansive newsroom of the *Boston Globe* in the USA. Photograph Stephen Quinn

this system was held at the Reform Club, where European correspondents met once a year. But when a new foreign editor arrived, the system 'more or less died immediately'. This illustrated the influence of senior editorial managers on knowledge management. As for dealing with the vast amount of data that entered the building, Brock admitted: 'I think if you looked at it as a cold, hard economist of data there is a lot of wastage. And a lot of effort is duplicated by people finding out things that are already known. But effective sharing depends on very, very good [and] robust user-friendly software. And very, very good [and] robust user-friendly software is a hell of a lot rarer than people think' (personal interview, London, 19 April 2001).

## New approaches for a new age

A new age requires new approaches – in terms of the management of both people and data. Given the importance of knowledge and information in the information age, and given the changing role of journalism within that environment, it is inevitable that structures have to change. But change takes time and often attracts resistance. Paul Saffo, director of the Institute for the Future in Menlo Park in California, works on what he calls the 30-year rule. He suggests that for the past 500 years it has taken about three decades for a new idea to 'fully seep into a culture' (1992: 18). New media commentator Roger Fidler notes that slowness of change is a 'rule rather than the exception' with emerging technologies. 'The 30-year rule may not be foolproof, but it does put the development of new technologies into a more realistic perspective' (Fidler, 1997: 10).

However, change is already happening in some newsrooms, especially in the USA and Asia. Chapter 3 shows that print journalists are being required to or asked to report for online and broadcast as well. Ifra's Kerry Northrup points out the integration is not moving along well in some editors' offices and news meetings. 'Rare is the newsroom where the online editor is a full participant in news decision-making or is running any primary news coverage. Rare is the news meeting where editors talk about the Web aspects of a story as readily as they deal with photos or graphics. Rare is the news editor who thinks of "the story" as something crossing media rather than just what will appear on the printed page, with all else being secondary. Rare is the chief editor who considers how a mix of print and new media might provide the most immediate impact on the community, rather than worrying mostly that the print rendition of the news not be scooped before it reaches readers many hours hence.' Northrup believes this is more an issue of mindset than workflow. 'And it remains one of the two biggest challenges in most newsrooms now that they have arrived in the twenty-first century' (Northrup, 2000a: 45). But change can happen fast.

Indeed, Northrup predicts that the situation is already changing and will change. 'More advanced newsrooms are working to develop hefty editorial knowledge bases of as many information resources as possible, and are implementing "virtual newsrooms" in which these information assets can be searched and accessed by any staff member from anywhere in the world over a robust editorial intranet. In essence, the network becomes the newsroom and the information/content flow over that network is the newspaper's lifeblood' (Northrup, 2000b: 14). Late in 2000 Northrup predicted that based on the current pace of innovation, multiple-media news handling should be 'predominant' some time in the first decade of the twenty-first century, and 'sooner for the really aggressive newsrooms' (2000b: 16). Chapter 3 studies the evolution and development of the multiple news operation. The next chapter considers what form the re-defined newsroom could and should adopt.

## How to learn more

1 Read books and Web sites about knowledge management and the role of knowledge in the information age. In particular, see Burton-Jones's *Knowledge Capitalism* (1999) and Karl-Erik Sveiby's Web site (http://www.sveiby.com.au).

2 Read the comprehensive list of articles on newsrooms in the Ifra archive. They can be found in the research section of the Ifra Web site (http://www.ifra.com).

3 Attend a conference or training session on knowledge management. See the Executive Information Systems Web site (http://www.dkms.com) for a list.

4 Read the monthly newsletter about information, *The Information Advisor*. Adobe portable document format (pdf) versions of the newsletter can be downloaded from the newsletter's Web site (http://www.informationadvisor.com).

5 Subscribe to Ifra's email-delivered *TrendReport*. Send a message to join-ifra-trendreport@kbx.de, but if you encounter problems or questions concerning your subscription send an email to trendreport@ifra.com. To read current editions of the newsletter online, visit the Ifra Web site (http://www.ifra.com/website/ifra.nsf/html/ITR).[nlr]

## References and further reading

Arnould, Valerie (2000) 'Finding the right approach to tackle a difficult issue'. *newspaper techniques*, May 2000, 44–46.

Australian Bureau of Statistics (2001) ABS catalogue number 3222.0.

Balding, Timothy (2001) 'World trends in the newspaper industry: An update'. Presentation to the World Association of Newspapers in Hong Kong, 4 June 2001.

Boyer, Tom (1999) 'Playing catch up'. *American Journalism Review*, July/August 1999, 47–51.

Burton-Jones, Alan (1999) *Knowledge Capitalism*. New York: Oxford University Press.

Chang, Dae-Whan (2001) 'Re-making a newspaper: *Maeil Business Newspaper* case'. A presentation to the World Association of Newspapers in Hong Kong, 5 June 2001.

Cortada, James (1998) 'Where did knowledge workers come from?' In J. Cortada, *Rise of the Knowledge Worker*. Boston: Butterworth-Heinemann.

Cramer, Chris (2001) 'Journalist, integrate thyself'. *The Guardian* 2 May 2001.

Fidler, Roger (1997) *Mediamorphosis: Understanding New Media*. Thousand Oaks CA: Pine Forge Press.

Franzini, Gabriella (2001) EidosMedia website http://www. eidosmedia.com.

Fulton, Katherine (2000) 'News isn't always journalism'. *Columbia Journalism Review*, July/August 2000.

Gates, Bill (1999) *Business @ the Speed of Thought: Succeeding in the Digital Economy*. New York: Penguin.

Gyllenhaal, Anders (2000) 'What's coming? Will we be ready for it?' An address to the Annual Association for Education in Journalism and Mass Communication, Pew Center, Washington, 10 August 2000. *Civic Catalyst*, 16–18.

*Ifra Trends 2001*, 'Latest trends in multiple media publishing'. Found at the Ifra Web site (http://www.ifra.com).

Johnson, J.T. 'Tom' (1994) 'Applied cybernetics and its implications for education for journalism'. *Australian Journalism Review*, July–December 1994, 16 (2), 55–66.

Johnson, J.T. 'Tom' (2001) Proposal for an Institute for Analytic Journalism. Personal interview in Boston, 22 April 2001. See http://mmcom.bu.edu/tjohnson/public/3fold.pdf.

Katz, Jon (2000) 'Can journalism survive technology?' In Kees, B., editor, *Recapture Your Youth: How to Create a Newspaper for Future Generations*. San Francisco: The Freedom Forum.

Kees, Beverly (2000) *Recapture Your Youth: How to Create a Newspaper for Future Generations*. San Francisco: The Freedom Forum.

Kilman, Larry (2001) 'World press trends: newspaper growth continues'. Press release issued by World Association of Newspapers, Hong Kong, 4 June 2001.

Landau, George (1999) 'Objects in mirror are closer than they appear'. In *When Nerds and Words Collide*, Paul, Nora, ed. Florida: Poynter Institute, 28–30.

Lane, Alan (2000) 'The age of knowledge frontier or fad?' *Communication World*, 1 June 2001. Includes the transcript of a seminar on knowledge management organized by the International Association of Business Communication.

McChesney, Robert (1999*) Rich Media, Poor Democracy: Communication Politics in Dubious Times.* Urbana: University of Illinois Press.

Miller, Stephen (1999) 'Journalists: turn around'. In *When Nerds and Words Collide*, Paul, Nora ed. Florida: Poynter Institute, 33–34.

Northrup, Kerry (1999) Presentation to the 'Newsroom for a Digital Age' conference, 7–8 December 1999, Darmstadt, Germany.

Northrup, Kerry (2000a) 'The third millennium has arrived, but is your newsroom ready for it?' *newspaper techniques*, January 2000, 44–45.

Northrup, Kerry (2000b) 'The redefined newsroom'. *newspaper techniques*, October 2000, 14–16.

Outing, Steve (2000) 'It's time to get serious about audio'. In Stop the Presses column, 1 November 2000. Found online at http://www.editorandpublisher.com/ephome/news/newshtm/ stop/st120600.htm

Pacific Area Newspaper Publishers' Association (PANPA) *Bulletin* (2000) 'World press trends show continued growth'. July 2000, 14–15.

PANPA *Bulletin* (2001) '10 years of newspaper growth'. May 2001, 10.

Rifkin, Jeremy (2000) *The End of Work: The Decline of the Global Work-force and the Dawn of the Post-market Era.* London: Penguin.

Roper, Dean (2000) 'Knowledge management – key to newspapers' transformation'. *newspaper techniques*, February 2000, 22–27.

Saffo, Paul (1992) 'Paul Saffo and the 30-year rule'. *Design World*, vol. 24.

Shannon, Claude and Weaver, Warren (1963) *The Mathematical Theory of Communication.* Illinois: University of Illinois Press.

Shenk, David (1997) *Data Smog: Surviving the Information Glut.* San Francisco: Harper Edge.

Shepard, Alicia (2000) 'Get big or get out'. *American Journalism Review*, March 2000, 22–29.

Smith, Terence (2001) 'News execs in a spot, media reporter says'. *USA Today* 18 June 2001, 4D.

Standage, Tom (1998) *The Victorian Internet.* New York: Walker and Company.

Sveiby, Karl-Erik (1996) 'Transfer of knowledge and the information processing professions'. *European Management Journal* 14 (4) August 1996, 379–88.

# 2  The re-defined newsroom

## Executive summary

Three major changes need to happen in the newsroom for knowledge management to evolve. The first and most important concerns the journalistic mindset and the way that journalists perceive their job. News is moving from being platform specific to a variety of forms because of consumer demand and changing lifestyles. Journalists need to be willing to change the way they work, and this initially requires a new way of looking at their role. The next change relates to the physical structure of the newsroom. Geography directly influences the flow of information and knowledge-age newsrooms need to look and work differently to facilitate that flow. The third change concerns the technology that journalists use and their attitude to it. Journalists need to accept the benefits of technology. At the same time, editorial managers need to see that technology is merely a tool for doing better journalism, and journalists need training to use these tools effectively. Overall, change must come from the top. This requires committed leadership and editorial managers willing to foster an environment that facilitates learning. Topics covered in this chapter include:

- ❑ attitude: changing newsroom mindsets
- ❑ links between technology and mindset
- ❑ blending competition and co-operation
- ❑ physical: moving the furniture around
- ❑ technical change: acceptance of technology
- ❑ from a production to an information base.

For knowledge management to flourish, change has to start in the engine-room of the information-driven organization – the newsroom. Media academic and analyst Beate Josephi notes that newsrooms are constantly changing: 'Their ongoing development is due to ever changing technology and economic parameters. Information about these changes is not only of use to the academy, but also the industry itself' (Josephi, 2000: 85). This chapter builds on that idea and explores the themes connected with change. These motifs fall into three categories – attitudinal, physical and technical – and will be discussed in that order. Attitude refers to changes in mindset and in the way that people perceive their role. Physical refers to new ways of structuring the newsroom. Technical links back to attitudinal because it relates both to the ways that people relate to the technology around them and to their actual adoption of it. People need to accept the benefits of technology before they use it effectively.

These three changes in turn necessitate alterations to newsroom workflow and organization. Leadership is central to all of these processes. The director of the Media Center at the American Press Institute, Andrew Nachison, believes journalists can learn to think and write for multiple platforms 'but it takes work, lots of training and leadership'. Nachison organizes the API's 'convergence tours' of Florida dailies and has been in an ideal position to observe the changes. 'Merging content is one thing. Merging cultures, values and organizations is another' (Nachison, 2001). The executive chairman of *Utusan* Melayu Berhad, Karamul Ariffin, attributes the major advances and changes at *Utusan* in Kuala Lumpur in Malaysia to the 'forward vision' of the board of directors and members of senior management. 'When our editor in chief discovered he could edit from far away places like Cuba we could not stem the tide of his enthusiasm' (Ariffin, 2001). *Utusan* is developing one of the world's first virtual newsrooms.

## Attitude: changing newsroom mindsets

Let's begin with attitudinal change, which relates to individual mindset and corporate culture. No one change is paramount, but this theme is the most common at all stages of the process. Several factors are related to a change in mindset, including a different attitude to time, a flexible approach to the journalistic role and a willingness to adopt more collaborative forms of work. Andrew Nachison quoted John Haile, the former editor of the *Orlando Sentinel*, who drove much of the convergence at the paper. Haile noted that managing change was difficult because it was necessary to 'change the way your people see themselves and do their jobs'. After implementing the changes, Haile left the paper to work as a partner with InsideOut Media.

The executive director of Ifra's Center for Advanced News Operations, Kerry Northrup, noted that speakers at a seminar on the newsroom for a digital age in December 1999 had one common theme – 'the battle over the newsroom's mindset'. He concluded that issues of attitude would be 'the toughest and most important battle to win in transitioning to a new newsroom'. Knowledge management was necessary to implement the kind of newsroom needed for multiple journalism, he said. This involved an 'overhaul' of the newsroom's attitude towards the information it handled and the knowledge it developed (1999). Northrup said serious implementation of knowledge management produced a major return on investment. '[It leads to] the development of really valuable assets, tangible assets – just like a building or a fleet of trucks – in the form of knowledge bases of information. Newspapers typically are not at [the] forefront of most technologies and true to their form, they are not at the forefront of knowledge management technologies. But the evolution cycle seems to be a lot faster now than it has been in past decades.' Newspapers were recognizing the increasing importance of being an information-based business rather than just a production-based business (personal interview with Northrup, Melbourne, 23 July 2000).

The deputy editor of Ifra's *newspaper techniques*, Brian Veseling, reporting on the same seminar, said speakers frequently mentioned flexibility as the key factor in successful change in the newsroom. 'If there is one word to describe what is being required more and more in newsrooms as journalism moves into the digital age it is flexibility. In an industry in which flexibility always has been an important element for success, it now seems to be vital for survival' (Veseling, 2000: 20). He was referring in part to the concept of multiple journalism, which is discussed in detail in the next chapter, but he also highlighted the need for a changed mindset for knowledge management to flourish.

The Newspaper Association of America's vice president for electronic media and industry development, Randy Bennett, believes newspapers must adapt to a dynamically changing marketplace. 'They dare not wait until certainty appears.' He predicted that newspapers would evolve to be 'truly multi-media companies' and organizational structures and process would change 'to make newspapers more nimble and responsive' (Bennett, 2000: 1–2).

The chief editor of Ming Pao Newspapers in Hong Kong, Paul Cheung, similarly believes the move to a multi-media environment can only be successful if accompanied by a corresponding change in the attitude of journalists. But the transformation must first occur in the minds of editorial managers: 'From my point of view, the chief editor has an important role. He must be a leader in terms of the changes.' Cheung saw the need to change attitudes – from the 'old' mindset to a multiple-media approach. 'We want them [journalists] to have the concept that news is news, whether it is printed or put online. Our journalists should try their best to package the news content according to the different medium. So it is a very challenging job, not only for me but also the new-generation journalists.' Cheung spent time using a form of 'helicopter vision' to plan for the changes. This is a management technique used to get above the daily work process to get an overview of where an organization needs to go. 'An editorial manager

must get above the daily process to see where they are going.'
Cheung said his aim was to create a new form of journalism.
'We are trying to develop a new breed of multi-media journalist. It takes time.' To manage the change of mindset,
Cheung felt it necessary to involve his staff. Between June and
December 1999 he held weekly meetings with senior editorial staff. He used these meetings to sell the new ideas: 'I aimed
to show my staff that the Net was the future and journalists
needed to change their approach to cope with it.' Cheung
admits there were some difficulties at first, but after discussion his staff saw the need for change and 'agreed to equip
themselves for the future'. Cheung argued in the meetings that
integrated journalism was a chance for *Ming Pao* journalists
to upgrade themselves. 'We are helping them to improve their
professional standing.' But the process needed time. 'It took
three to six months for the process to evolve. Corporate culture plays a very important role in convergence. My staff are
not the highest paid in Hong Kong but they believe in what
they are doing' (personal interview, Hong Kong, 7 June 2001;
also quoted in Loh, 2000). *Ming Pao* recruited its new journalists online – applications had to be made via email. No
postal address was given in advertisements. Cheung called
this a natural process of elimination (quoted in Loh, 2000:
47).

Ifra writer Valerie Arnould noted in her interviews with
French multi-media journalists that their attitude to time had
similarly changed. She quoted Atlantel (http://www.
atlantel.fr) editor-in-chief Anne Briolais: 'Journalists working
in a multi-media press company have to keep in mind that
information on the Web or on audio-visual media is output in
real time. The deadlines that used to apply when completing
articles for a daily paper are well and truly over' (Arnould,
2000: 46). Cheung points out that a major change associated
with a multiple-media newsroom is the need to work around
the clock. 'The operation changes completely.' During a trial
of Ming Pao's 'instant news' service, journalists had to work
with five deadlines – at 04:00 h, 09:00 h, 13:00 h, 17:00 h and
21:00 h. 'That means at every deadline we need to send some

fresh or updated news items online. This is a new culture that we have to adapt to together with all our journalists' (quoted in Loh, 2000: 48).

Andrew Nachison, director of API's Media Center, said significant operational and strategic challenges arose during the process of 'morphing' from a single-platform operation to a multiple-media system. One of the most important was the need to manage the change itself, and to help people in the organization to commit to the purpose of a multi-media news company. But the challenge was not limited to the newsroom, he said. Sales, marketing and even support staff needed to come to grips with what the enterprise was all about. 'All media have developed standards, traditions and even language, and convergence at times involves abandoning decades of learned behavior and attitudes. For instance, newspaper reporters have long focused on a single deadline, typically early evening for a morning newspaper. Television reporters have to move more quickly to get the same story on the evening news. Today, those same reporters may have to provide short text or even complete text or video packages hours sooner to meet the demands of a never-ending 24-hour news cycle.' Nachison pointed out that the 24-hour news cycle was not new. 'Wire service reporters have been working comfortably with it for years, and they are trained to understand that the news must get out. The information is the driver, not the delivery platform. That's the lesson that can be most difficult to learn: that the newspaper, television station or Web site you once thought you worked exclusively for is no longer your priority. You are no longer exclusive to any platform. Your priority is getting the information out on whatever platform it should be on.' Helping people accept this 'new world view' takes time, training, executive leadership and money, Nachison said. 'It's a simple transformation for some, and more difficult for others. If you became a newspaper writer because you cherished the time it afforded for reporting, reflection and carefully crafted stories, the new world of convergence may not suit you – even if you're good at it' (Nachison, 2001).

Northrup labels organizations that apply knowledge management techniques and encourage flexible mindsets as 'smart newsrooms'. They work as 'a collective journalistic mind' rather than as a collection of individual editorial thinkers. 'Think: Two heads are better than one – or in a newsroom's case, 25, 50, 100 or 200 heads probably have something to contribute to newsroom decision-making' (Northrup, 1999). In some respects this is an application of the work of management consultant Peter Senge, famous for his book *The Fifth Discipline* (1990), who notes that better decisions come from teams rather than individuals. A smart newsroom involved as many people as possible in making news judgements, Northrup said, 'because it is smart to make use of the vast experience and perspective you have already paid to assemble on the editorial floor'. Through collaboration, organizations discover stories that individuals had not thought of, along with better ways of pursuing and presenting stories. 'It might mean for instance making sure that a comprehensive list of working stories is widely distributed for everyone's information – or better yet, having the list maintained and constantly updated online for real-time access and comment by anyone. It might involve broadcasting news meetings to television sets around the newsroom and over the editorial intranet to remote locations.' Northrup said several newspapers were experimenting with projecting information onto walls or electronic tickers that 'put story assignments, changes and status up there for everyone's edification'. Modern communication and collaboration tools permit fuller participation 'without the organizational overhead and committee lag time that a deadline newsroom cannot afford' (1999). *Ming Pao* in Hong Kong displays the news budget at its main news conference by projecting a Word file onto a wall. A digital file is easier to modify than a paper list.

## Links between technology and mindset

The executive chairman of the *Utusan* group in Malaysia, Kamarul Ariffin, said *Utusan* had managed to convert successfully to a virtual newsroom because of his workforce's ability to adapt to change. The company's virtual editorial project was more than half completed and would be operating fully by the end of 2002, he said. During the transition, staff were 'above all conditioning ourselves to the modern digital age'. Ariffin attributed the success of the move to the 'forward vision' of the board of directors and members of senior management, the presence of effective communication facilities, the availability of necessary technology and the willingness of the workforce to 're-learn and adapt to changes'. 'All these helped to contribute to the speedy acceptance of the virtual editorial system' (Ariffin, 2001). CNN.com's Asia–Pacific news director, John Beeston, believes that effecting cultural change is more difficult than introducing new technology. At the end of 2000, CNN placed 20 new multi-media journalists in CNN's TV newsroom in Hong Kong. 'It was an interesting process,' Beeston said. 'We decided to tackle the challenge head on. It would have been easy to place the new starters on a separate floor and attempt the integration slowly through shared editorial meetings. However the judgement was made to sit all the journalists together, indeed mix them up into areas of speciality so that the dot-com business [journalists] sat with TV business [journalists] and the dot-com news [journalists] with TV news [journalists]. The benefit of this system was a fast integration of people and ideas. The downside was potential open warfare. I'm happy to report that it worked well to the point that we are now one CNN in Hong Kong, with one managing editor.' How did he get his staff involved? 'You've got to get people to buy in, get them excited. And you've got to trust your staff. News is organic. It's impossible to run a newsroom like a military operation. You have to give people their freedom and get on with the job' (Beeston, 2001).

Allan Marshall, group technology director for Associated Newspapers Ltd in London, said it was essential to make a fundamental change – a paradigm shift – in the way news organizations work. 'It's clear that the current electronic revolution is something more than just a new competitor. Its implications run wider and deeper than the earlier challenges of radio and television. Superficially it offers similar threats – new ways of disseminating news, information, entertainment and sport. Underneath it offers a wealth of opportunities for developing and enhancing our core businesses – *if* we are willing to take them' (Marshall, 2001).

The president of the NewsEngin company, George Landau, similarly noted the link between technology and mindset. He said the newspaper industry must move beyond the thinking that technology involved a pagination system. 'The industry may need to rethink the newsroom entirely.' Landau maintains that any new start-up should choose an application platform first, and choose it carefully. This platform should establish a 'software foundation' for all applications. 'We would deploy a platform that doesn't force the staff to take sides in the Wintel-Mac debate' (quoted in Cole, 2001). New media commentator Steve Outing predicted that the first few years of the twenty-first century would be 'difficult' for news companies. Major cultural shifts would be required in newsrooms as employees and managers adopted the notion that they no longer operated just a newspaper or television station. 'And if you doubt that this transformation will occur, consider this: Media giant NBC recently told all of its employees to cancel their print newspaper subscriptions whenever possible and instead get all of their news online. What this anecdote says is that the modern news company must disseminate its product (news and information) to many different media platforms – with print being only one, and many other formats being digital' (Outing, 2001).

## Blending competition and co-operation

One aspect of a change in mindset is the move towards 'co-opertition' among media organizations. Co-opertition is an amalgam of competition and co-operation and represents a new form of business in which organizations that originally were competitors work together when it suits each party.

Walter Keichel, editor of the *Harvard Business Review*, said the essence of the theory could be reduced to two sentences: 'Co-operate with others to increase the size of the pie. Compete in cutting it up.' But he inserted a cautionary note: 'The others with whom you may wish to co-operate could include businesses with which you compete on other fronts' (Keichel, 2001). When the Australian trade-promotion group Austrade and *The Australian Financial Review* sponsored a trade mission to Silicon Valley in October 1998, the ten electronic commerce companies on the tour were on guard against each other. To some of them, the concept of 'co-operatition' was a revelation, reporter David Crowe noted. Australian companies needed to 'jettison' their insularity: 'Entrepreneurs must hook into a networked world where the willingness to swap tips overrides jealousy about a rival's progress, where even direct competitors engage more openly than they would in Australia' (Crowe, 1998: 30).

Newspaper consultant John Morton noted that the media world was seeing concentrations of ownership that would have been unthinkable two decades earlier. For example, *The Washington Post* and *Newsweek* (part of the same company) shared news stories with NBC Television News and MSNBC.com (the latter itself an alliance between the TV network and the Microsoft Corporation). *The Wall Street Journal* developed a similar sharing arrangement with CNBC, the business channel of the NBC television network. Further alliances between news operations owned by separate and often competing entities was inevitable, he concluded. 'The rules have been changed by the globalization of business and, especially for media companies, the rise of the Internet. Newspapers had no choice, he said, 'but to plunge in' (Morton, 2000: 88). *The Daily Telegraph* reported in May 2001 that it had joined forces with three other leading European newspapers to form an alliance to encourage co-operation between the papers and their Web sites. The European Dailies Alliance comprised *Die Welt* in Germany, *Le Figaro* in France, *ABC* in Spain along with *The Daily Telegraph* in Britain. All would help each others' correspondents and share content. The telegraph.co.uk Web site would provide direct links to the Web sites of its colleagues and they would link directly to its site.

## Physical: moving the furniture around

The newsroom of the future will have re-arranged furniture. That's how Northrup summarized one aspect of the altered mindset. 'The future of newsrooms is apparently round. Not always perfectly round. Sometimes it looks more oval, or egg shaped, or even a bit like a squashed pineapple. Nevertheless, at newspapers all over the world, editors are re-arranging furniture to get rid of long straight rows of desks, isolated corners of journalists and narrow aisles of thinking about how a newsroom should look' (Northrup, 2000a: 55). The theoretical work behind the movement of the furniture is based on the work of architect Saf Fahim of New York. He believes that structures influence the way people operate. Indeed, art theorist John Berger has long maintained that the environment in which people work and live influences their attitudes and habits. He cites the example of how people keep their voices low while in church or a library, but cheer loudly while at a football stadium – showing that the physical environment impacts directly on how people behave (Berger, 1972: 23–24). Architect Saf Fahim has been designing newsrooms since the early 1990s. He believes that traditional newsrooms inhibit creative thinking. After visiting scores of newsrooms in nine countries, this author agrees. Newsrooms display a conspicuous level of similarity. Desks of a uniform drab beige or grey are grouped in pods, cubicles or rows. A terminal sits on each desk, suggesting that technology or the IT staff determine where people sit. Seating should instead reflect people's information needs.

In 1992 the Associated Press invited Fahim to study the work environment of newspapers across the USA to see how work methods could be improved. He spent two years on the project. In 1997 Fahim told a conference organized by the

American Society of Newspaper Editors (ASNE) about the similarities he observed in the work processes of journalists and architects. But he also noted that journalists' environments did not encourage the creative thinking vital to their work. Their newsrooms resembled assembly lines that stifled creative juices. 'Most importantly, it [the newsroom] does not help you manage stress. There is a lot of stress in newsrooms and news organizations, and the space [environment] itself does not encourage you to manage it.'

Fahim runs Archronica Architects in New York. He has worked with the School of Mass Communications at the University of South Carolina at Columbia to design the Newsplex newsroom of the future, discussed in chapter 5 (Figures 2.1 and 2.2). Fahim's ideal newsroom has an amphitheatre in the centre for news meetings. It is designed so that anyone in the organization can listen to the meetings, to share ideas. Readers would also be invited into the building to talk to reporters and editors about the issues of the day. Fahim envisions newsrooms with large, open spaces that seat numerous employees – again, to encourage the free exchange of ideas. Smaller areas could be used for smaller groups such as a team of four or five editors, to brainstorm ideas. These areas include movable desks because people need to be able to change their seating patterns to perform different jobs. Large areas are valuable for promoting discussion and making decisions, but once an action plan has been established, it was then best for reporters and editors to have private areas, Fahim said. These small and enclosed individual workspaces were aimed at providing journalists with the private time and space they needed for critical thinking and concentration as they worked on writing stories or editing and designing pages. Once their stories or pages were finished, Fahim said, the journalists would return to areas that were open and accessible so that others can critique their work. This happens in a small way at some daily newspapers, where the section front pages of the previous day are displayed at the morning news conference to encourage feedback. But it happens after the paper appears. Fahim's approach is to invoke collaboration as part of the creative process. In Fahim's ideal environment, recreation areas will incorporate open spaces designed to counter stress, so employees return to work with renewed energy. The traditionally dingy newspaper cafeteria would be replaced with elegant coffee bars and other pleasant environments (Fahim, 2001). The person who introduced Fahim at the 1997 ASNE conference, Tonnie Katz, editor of *The Orange County Register* in Santa Ana, California, said Fahim was not talking about putting a new engine in our old car. 'He is talking about building a new factory that can make any product we want, even things we haven't thought about yet.'

Jim Foundy, editor of the *Daily Hampshire Gazette* in Northampton, Massachusetts, attended that ASNE conference and wrote about the experience (1997). Fahim had found that journalists were 'nice people who do not work in nice places'

**Figure 2.1** The large display monitors envisaged by architect Saf Fahim are designed to show the progress of pages as they are assembled. Image courtesy of Archronica Architects, New York

**Figure 2.2** An artist's impression of the environment that information-age journalists could expect in the newsroom of the future. Image courtesy of Archronica Architects, New York

and proposed to rebuild organizations to foster dialogue and mutual understanding among departments, and between the organization and its readers. Foundy noted that most editors would probably never see a newsroom with the airiness and atmosphere sketched by Fahim, but 'there was no disputing' the core of his message: 'A changing newspaper industry needs to tear down departmental barriers, talk more with readers, and break out of potential-limiting boxes'. Brian Veseling of *newspaper techniques* concurred: 'Without question the newsrooms that will thrive today and in the future are going to look and operate much differently from the ones of yesterday' (2000: 20). Northrup analysed traditional newsrooms and concluded that they were usually divided into work areas matching progressive steps in the production process – writing followed by editing and design. But tomorrow's newsroom will organizationally be built around phases in an information flow. 'The major "desks" will be those that handle activities such as story development, content co-ordination, news coverage and content creation, media-specific presentation/distribution, reader interaction and editorial information management/technology.' Northrup concluded that editorial managers would probably need to produce departmental descriptions that were 'more appealing to the journalistic ethic' (2000b: 48).

A feature of the converged newsroom is a central desk from where key editorial staff co-ordinate news coverage. Specialist reporters and support staff work from desks arranged around the central desk. Three of the most ambitious examples can be found in Florida in the USA. The Media General communications group spent a reported US$40 million to co-locate its newspaper, the *Tampa Tribune*, with a television station and online enterprise that it also owns in the same market. About 140 km away in the same state, the Tribune company has put together its version of synergy by locating the *Orlando Sentinel* on a 'campus' with its online edition, a television channel and some radio stations all within walking distance of each other. Elsewhere in Florida, the Sarasota *Herald-Tribune* launched a 24-hour local cable news channel, in partnership with Comcast Cable, in 1995. It started its Web site in 1997. The next chapter provides details of these and other forms of converged newsrooms.

Gil Thelen, executive editor of the *Tampa Tribune*, describes his building as the 'Taj Mahal of newsrooms'. It occupies four floors on the west bank of the Hillsborough River, and it is filled with the latest digital technologies. 'We have nothing analog in the house any more.' Placing all editorial teams in the same building was part of the essence of convergence, along with the centralized news desk: 'Geography is destiny in this game'. Thelen referred to a 'new energy' in the building. The *Tampa Tribune* had a quicker and better newsroom because of the changes. He attributed this directly to the *Tampa Tribune*'s 'editorial muscle' of more than 300 journalists, 120 of whom were reporters. The print publication supplied a sense of security for the television newsroom. As a consequence, the television news produced at partner WFLA-TV was deeper and more contextual. This in turn had produced a ratings boom for the station. 'The daily breaking news collaboration is increasing exponentially and the cultural accommodation is also working well.' Convergence was driven by market fragmentation, the growth of the Web and changing lifestyles where people wanted information on demand, Thelen said. He noted that an early and important part of his role was changing the mindset in the newsroom and getting people to see that their core journalistic ingredient was news and information – it did not matter in what form they delivered it (personal interview with Thelen, Washington, 8 June 2000).

The *Orlando Sentinel* has also devised a multiple-media desk for co-ordinating news. Staff call the circular newsdesk the 'Starship' because of its curved shape and the way the position of the desk's computers remind them of the bridge of the Starship Enterprise in the *Star Trek* television series. Associate managing editor for content development, Steve Doyle, noted that the desk provided a location for all the organization's editorial decision-makers. It allowed the individuals in a complex operation to work together efficiently. Editors for the print, online, radio and cable TV operations worked alongside production staff. When a major story broke, the aim was to cover it in as many formats as possible and practical. Photographers carried still and video cameras. As of mid-2000, about one-third of the newsroom's 360 print journalists had been trained to appear on air. Reporters usually wrote early versions of a story for the Web edition and later completed a longer story for print (personal interview with Steve Doyle, Washington, 8 June 2000). One of the editors, John Huff, noted that the Starship was a constant reminder to staff that things were changing in news publishing and that they needed to change as well (quoted in Northrup, 2000a: 56).

Northrup reports that major newsroom changes also have occurred at the *Birmingham Evening Mail* in England. Editor-in-chief Ian Dowell said the changes were 'not about technology' but about the way people worked. 'Among the more revolutionary changes devised by a committee the journalists themselves set up was elimination of all sub-editors. Accountability for quality and accuracy of text is now placed squarely on the shoulders of reporters and their news editors, whose ranks were strengthened by some of the re-assigned copy subs.' This is a relatively common practice in continental Europe. One of Germany's most prestigious newspapers, the *Frankfurter Allgemeine Zeitung* (*FAZ*), also does not have sub-editors, but expects the section editors to check copy. It organizes news coverage via specialized desks. Dr Klaus Viedebantt, a former editor of the home desk who looks after the paper's trainees, said story length was left to reporters to decide: 'They know their subject and they are specialists, so we expect them to know how much or how little to write'. The *FAZ* is based in Germany's financial capital and is the country's paper of record for politics and economics. It has a highly educated staff (personal interview with Klaus Viedebantt, Frankfurt, 25 April 2001).

At the *Birmingham Evening Mail*, sub-editors were retrained and re-designated as page planners, with much more active presentation responsibility than just piecing together components of pages like a jigsaw puzzle on deadline. Northrup noted that the basis of the change was a redesigned newsroom: 'Desks cover the big open floor in a kind of interlocking helix, reminiscent of a chemical DNA diagram. When one looks down on the newsroom from the raised observation hall, there are discernible groupings, such as where all the reporters sit, regardless of whether they are news or features writers. All the page editors are together too, making it easier for them to switch around on any section, any page and any topic as needed. But the overall impression is that there are no isolated clusters of people, no opportunity for independent newsrooms to form within the newsroom and no invitation for a staff member to be cut off from the collective news effort.' At the core of this curving editorial helix sat the four key co-ordinators, said head of news Steve Dyson. These were the news editor and deputy news editor, the chief page planner and the production editor, who was also the page one editor. They sat across from each other and within sight of everyone else in the room, and essentially ran a non-stop news meeting. Observed Northrup: 'No issue of newsgathering, story selection or production – print or electronic – is outside their collective authority and responsibility. Editors and reporters need bring questions and problems nowhere else to get a resolution'. Dyson said the project was designed to create a newsroom that emphasized quality and flexibility. Along the way it also created a newsdesk that would serve as the forerunner for a multiple-media news organization (Northrup, 2000a: 55). *The Times* in England has combined its newspaper newsdesk with the online newsdesk.

In Australia, *The Age* in Melbourne also decided to move its furniture around, as part of a major programme to get more analysis into the paper (Figure 2.3). The move occurred on the weekend of 3–4 March 2001. Ken Merrigan, sections editor, said the process was designed to get more reporters' copy in the paper and not so much agency material, because the former was more unique. The physical manifestation of this process involved the establishment of a central news desk, and locating the online news editor alongside the newspaper equivalent. 'It's part of a move to deeper reporting. We decided we need to marshal our resources more efficiently, and we have a need for greater specialization among reporters.'

Editor and associate publisher Michael Gawenda summarized the approach in a memo to staff: 'We don't cover everything but what we cover we do better than anyone else'. News in future would be agenda-driven and not based on a 'wish-list' of what appeared at the morning conference, with its four pages of everything that might be covered, Merrigan said (2001). The new format also showed the need for collaboration and new roles. Gawenda appointed two key staff to the centralized news desk: a deputy editor for breaking news and a deputy editor for news packages. James Button fills the latter role. His job is to identify important news items of the day and compile a 'package' of information about them. This includes analysis, opinion and background information – areas in which newspapers can provide something for their readers that other media cannot. 'People are saturated with news. There's the Internet, there's radio and there's TV. We can't just tell people what's happened. We have to say why things have happened and that's the job of newspapers, I think ... We live in an increasingly pluralistic society. It throws up the dilemma for a paper of how to speak to this incredibly differentiated group of people. So our task is to write more stories that are analytical, that are entertaining and that tell narratives about things to all people' (Button, 2001: 1–3). Figures 2.3 and 2.4 show the revised *Age* news-desk from different angles.

Production processes have also changed. Instead of writing followed by editing, the two processes more closely parallel each other. This new approach required an earlier news con-

**Figure 2.3** In March 2001 *The Age* in Melbourne moved the furniture around so that the news desk for the print edition works with that of the online edition. Photograph Stephen Quinn

**Figure 2.4** Another view of the news desk at *The Age* in Melbourne. Photograph Stephen Quinn

ference to organize effective coverage of the major events of the day. Improved co-ordination between the news desk and the production sub-editors was also needed. Merrigan said the catalyst for change was a visit from Ifra's Kerry Northrup in May 2000. A group of senior *Age* staff absorbed Northrup's report and held a mini retreat in a Melbourne hotel. 'We asked the question: How are papers to evolve for the new century?' said Merrigan. Over time, he had noticed a 'road to Damascus' conversion among senior editorial managers. The process had highlighted a need for better planning. 'Journalists have deluded themselves into thinking it was fine to be spontaneous with news coverage. But what we need is better planning. And we need to query our historical attitudes about how we cover news. So much news is predictable. We get comfortable with patterns when we should be using patterns to our advantage and planning more. We also need to be flexible, to be able to respond to major breaking news, such as fires, emergencies or police stories. And we need to work better in teams' (personal interview, Melbourne, 1 March 2001).

The chief editor of Ming Pao Newspapers, Paul Cheung, noted that major refurbishment had taken place to prepare for his organization's move to a multiple-media platform. The fourteenth floor of the Ming Pao Building was converted into a multiple-media newsroom, to house the television studio and the online groups. These included mingpao.com and its various portals and the online development units. The fourteenth floor was chosen because it was close to the newspaper newsrooms on the sixteenth floor. Corporate offices and conference rooms occupy the fifteenth. Cheung integrated many of the teams on the newspaper and online editions by requiring them to sit with each other. Business reporters at the online and newspaper sections, for example, have a combined editor and sit together on the fourteenth floor. A state-of-the-art digital studio sits next to the combined desk. It has three remote-controlled cameras, operated by a two-person studio crew. Staff appreciate the convenience of having desks and studio so close to each other (personal interview with Cheung, Hong Kong, 7 June 2001; also quoted in Loh, 2000).

Collaboration via working in teams is one of the key changes needed for the information age, and is discussed in chapter 4. Newsroom managers have to overcome the tendency towards individual effort in newsrooms. The 'lone wolf' may be a nice aspect of journalistic mythology but new eras require new approaches. Most management theory agrees that many heads are always better than one in improving the decision-making process. Journalists need to be more willing to share and chapter 4 suggests that intranets provide one way to improve the possibility of sharing. Experienced reporters have vast amounts of useful knowledge in their heads but its potential is wasted if it remains locked up. Journalists must be willing to store and distribute their knowledge. The modern newspaper will need to provide a platform of services, with information as its core component. One way to do that is with the myriad technology available to newsrooms.

## Technical change: acceptance of technology

The third change outlined in the introduction to this chapter involves journalists' adoption and acceptance of technology. In the last three decades of the twentieth century, almost all news organizations have embraced the digital revolution. They began with 'dumb terminals', though most journalists used them as little more than electronic typewriters (McKercher, 1996). Papers followed this with pagination, which allowed sub-editors and designers direct control over composition. The down side there was that too many editors spent too much time building pages rather than editing stories. Similarly, digital cameras and the ability to scan negatives offered new ways to do photo-journalism. But lack of planning or insufficient disk space meant that it was difficult to archive all the images (Northrup, 1996). From the 1970s, digital wire service feeds and satellite technology meant that journalists could receive huge amounts of data quickly. But in many respects this volume of data has proved too much to handle (see the information overload section in the previous chapter). It was often too difficult to archive the fresh material flooding into the newsroom each day. Reporters were given laptops so they could write from remote sites but inadequate communications links made it increasingly difficult to co-ordinate staff. And then the Internet arrived. It has become difficult to index or account for the massive amounts of data available on the Web. Professor Peter Verwey has noted that since the end of World War II the world's supply of information had grown 10 per cent but our ability to consume it had only grown by 3.5 per cent. Professor Luciano Floridi has argued that we are losing our way in the human encyclopaedia. The Internet, he says, 'resembles a huge library where every half hour a new load of books is dumped in the doors and every day they change the position of the books on the shelves' (Quinn, 1999: 9).

Northrup summarized the difficulties elegantly: the late twentieth century had produced 'a newsroom full of digital technology – and full of digital problems'. Technology had been applied piecemeal to editorial structures, and workflows had not been designed to make the best use of the new tools available to journalists. Technology has also been focused on isolated production tasks rather than on the more fundamental issues of managing information flow and newsroom staff. In the rush to introduce digital technology, most newsrooms had not supplied the necessary infrastructure. 'Being digital is not just a state of technology. It is a way of thinking, a way of defining the critical processes that make up a news operation, and a way of linking those processes to make the newsroom more dynamic. It means using technology more effectively, not just using more technology' (Northrup, 1996: 4). Northrup was referring to the necessary change of mindset discussed earlier in this chapter. He believes the newsroom of the future must make more astute use of technology and foresees a time when reporters will routinely work in the field with mobile phones and portable digital assistants such as the Palm Pilot. Newsrooms will consequently become smaller, with fewer people based at the headquarters on a daily basis. 'More advanced newsrooms are working to develop hefty editorial knowledge bases of as many information resources as possible, and are implementing "virtual newsrooms" in which these information assets can be searched and accessed by any staff member from anywhere in the world over a robust editorial intranet. In essence, the network becomes the newsroom and the information/content flow over that network is the newspaper's lifeblood' (Northrup, 2000c: 14). For editorial managers, information management, communication and staff co-ordination will become 'major portions of their jobs' (Northrup, 2000b: 49). Once managers decide on the primacy of information and knowledge in the reporting role, they will need to consider the types of technology to make available to journalists. Chapters 5 and 6 discuss these tools. This section of this chapter looks more at journalists' attitudes to, and adoption of, technology.

Media historian Anthony Smith has noted that every new technological device – for example, the telegraph, typewriter or telephone – tended to act as the 'defining catalyst' for the emergence of a 'new brand of journalism' (1977: 186). The devices need not be mechanical, they could also relate to a special skill 'not directly related to a piece of machinery' (1978: 213). The role of the reporter in the early to mid-nineteenth century, for example, demanded a range of new skills that included powers of observation, validation of statements and the rapid and accurate recording of information acquired. Acquisition of new skills such as Pitman shorthand from about the 1850s produced what Smith described as 'a new era' in reporting (1977: 185–87). 'With the coming of Pitman and the first easily acquired and transferable shorthand system, a new era in reporting was brought about' (1978: 214). Margaret DeFleur echoed Smith when she described computer-assisted reporting (CAR) as 'a specialized area of study' within journalism that introduced 'an important new era in the history of the press' (1994: 5–6). Chapter 5 discusses new tools and forms of reporting. Noted Smith: '[Reporters] are constantly re-professionalized to new tasks, as each formulation of a medium succeeds its predecessor'. Such will be the case with the digital tools available to journalists, increasing the need for awareness and practice of knowledge-management techniques.

## From a production to an information base

Northrup correctly asserts that newsrooms must become information based, rather than production based. Journalism must become an information-age profession rather than an industrial-age trade. Because of the link between technology and information, news organizations will continually need to update gear for managing news. But central to the change will be the content database where journalists store and update their multiple-media packages. Production journalists at their desks would simply take from this database the elements needed for a particular presentation. 'So the critical central function becomes the content co-ordination', Northrup concluded (2000b: 49). This will entail the need for a new kind of journalist, capable of managing diverse news flows and seeing multiple-journalism possibilities as news breaks. Increasingly, technology will also become available to reduce the amount of time senior editorial staff spend in meetings. 'Another advantage of the completely integrated communications capabilities in tomorrow's newsroom – such as instant video-conferencing – is that meetings can be held without requiring all the attendees to get up and go to a meeting area. People can join the meeting virtually and get just as much out of it without the disruption of having to leave their work areas and walk someplace else and then return later.' Face-to-face meetings would still be needed, Northrup admits. But the trend towards more virtual participation would allow four or five editors to work out an issue in two minutes and then go their separate ways – rather than 'dealing with the scheduling and relocation hassles that would invariably turn a small planning session into a 20- or 30-minute time waster' (2000b: 49). The Newspaper Association of America's Randy Bennett believes a major challenge for newspaper companies will be the need to find, recruit and retain 'technology-savvy personnel'. By 'savvy' he means people 'who are not wedded to one medium and are comfortable working with technology' (2000: 1). Chapter 7 discusses this issue. The next chapter traces the evolution of multiple-journalism in newsrooms on several continents and suggests it is an integral and early part of the evolution of knowledge management in the modern news organization.

## How to learn more

1 Subscribe to *newspaper techniques*, Ifra's monthly magazine. It is published in five languages. Details can be found at the Ifra home page (http://www.ifra.com). In particular read anything by Kerry Northrup.

2 Obtain a copy of Ifra's video *Tomorrow's News*, available free on CD. Copies can be requested from Ifra by email to Astrid Luecker at luecker@ifra.com. The French and Spanish versions can be obtained from Vincent Peyrègne at

peyregne@ifra.com. The movie can now also be viewed
online courtesy of PubliGroupe (http://www.publi-
groupe.com). For very high-speed connections (500 Kbits/
second) go to: atrtsp://streaming.publigroupe.com/mcon-
nect/IfraNewsRoom_High.rm; for high-speed connections
(such as ADSL) go to rtsp://streaming.publigroupe.
com/mconnect/ IfraNewsRoom.rm; and for 56K modem
connections go to rtsp://streaming.publigroupe.com/
mconnect/IfraNewsRoom_Low.rm

3 Support Professor Tom Johnson's Institute for Analytical
Journalism. Details can be found at http://mmcom.bu.
edu/tjohnson/public/3fold.pdf[nlr]

## References and further reading

American Society of Newspaper Editors annual conference, 9 April
1997 entitled 'Ways to encourage breakthrough thinking'.
Transcript found at http://www.asne.org/kiosk/archive/con-
vention/conv97/breakthroughthinking.htm.

Ariffin, Kamarul (2001) 'Virtual editorial: *Utusan*'s experience'. A
presentation to the World Newspaper Association's annual conference in Hong Kong, 5 June 2001.

Arnould, Valerie (2000) 'Finding the right approach to tackle a difficult issue'. *newspaper techniques*, May 2000, 44–46.

Beeston, John (2001) 'CNN Hong Kong: the digital news room'.
Presentation to the World Association of Newspapers in Hong
Kong, 5 June 2001.

Bennett, Randy (2000) 'Horizon watching: seizing new opportunities'. Paper presented to Ifra's 'Beyond the Printed Word' conference, Amsterdam, 9–12 October 2000.

Berger, John (1972) *Ways of Seeing*. London: British Broadcasting
Corporation; Harmondsworth: Penguin.

Button, James (2001). Personal interview in Melbourne, 1 March
2001. Also quoted in *Inside The Age* (author anonymous),
February 2001, 1–3.

Cole, David (2001) 'Digital visions: the completely electronic workflow'. *Presstime*, February 2001.

Crowe, David (1998) 'The secret of sharing success in Silicon Valley'.
*The Australian Financial Review*, 28 November 1998, 30.

Cunningham, Brent (2000) 'The AP now'. *Columbia Journalism Review*, November/December 2000.

*Daily Telegraph* (2001) 'Europe's top newspapers come together'. 9 May 2001.

DeFleur, Margaret (1994) 'The development and methodology of computer-assisted investigative reporting'. PhD Thesis, Syracuse University, USA.

DeFleur, Margaret (1997) *Computer-Assisted Investigative Reporting*. New Jersey: Lawrence Erlbaum Associates.

Fahim, Saf (2001) Presentation to the World Association of Newspapers in Hong Kong, 5 June 2001. Also personal communication 5 June 2001.

Foundy, Jim (1997) 'Institutional innovation key to staying current'. Report on ASNE conference, found at http://www.asne.org/kiosk/editor/97.june/foudy1.htm.

Josephi, Beate (2000) 'Newsroom research: its importance for journalism studies'. *Australian Journalism Review*, 22 (2), 75–87.

Keichel, Walter (2001) 'Co-opetition true and false: an alternative to convergence?'. Presentation to the World Association of Newspapers in Hong Kong, 6 June 2001.

Loh, Peter (2000) 'Credibility of content guides Ming Pao's move to multiple media'. *newspaper techniques*, December 2000, 46–48.

Marshall, Allan (2001) Presentation to the Information and Communications Technology Round Table, World Association of Newspapers in Hong Kong, 3 June 2001.

McKercher, Catherine (1996) 'Computers and reporters: newsroom practices at two Canadian daily newspapers'. *Canadian Journal of Communication* 20 (2).

Morton, John (2000) 'The emergence of convergence'. *American Journalism Review*, January–February 2000, 88.

Nachison, Andrew (2001) 'Good business or good journalism? Lessons from the bleeding edge'. A presentation to the World Editors' Forum, Hong Kong, 5 June 2001. Also email communication 12 June 2001.

Northrup, Kerry (1996) 'The digital newsroom of the future: a new way of managing the news'. *The Seybold Report on Publishing Systems*, 25 (18), 3–8.

Northrup, Kerry (1999) Presentation to the Newsroom for a Digital Age conference, 7–8 December 1999, Darmstadt, Germany.

Northrup, Kerry (2000a) 'Future newsrooms mean re-arranging the furniture'. *PANPA Bulletin*, April 2000, 55–56.

Northrup, Kerry (2000b) 'Exploring the look and layout of tomorrow's newsroom'. *newspaper techniques*, April 2000, 48–49.

Northrup, Kerry (2000c) 'The redefined newsroom'. *newspaper techniques* October 2000, 14–16.

Outing, Steve (2001) 'Mixing old and new media', *Editor & Publisher Online*, 31 January 2001.

Quinn, Stephen (1999) *Newsgathering on the Net*. Melbourne: Macmillan.

Senge, Peter (1990) *The Fifth Discipline: The Art and Practice of the Learning Organization*. New York: Doubleday/Currency.

Smith, Anthony (1977) 'Technology and control: the interactive dimensions of journalism'. In Curran, Gurevitch and Woollacott, editors, *Mass Communication and Society*. London: Edward Arnold.

Smith, Anthony (1978) *The Politics of Information: Problems of Policy in Modern Media*. London: Macmillan.

Smith, Anthony (1979) *The Newspaper: An International History*. London: Thames and Hudson.

Smith, Anthony (1980) *Goodbye Gutenberg: The Newspaper Revolution of the 1980s*. New York and Oxford: Oxford University Press.

Veseling, Brian (2000) 'Flexibility the key in the multi-media world'. *PANPA Bulletin*, November 2000, 20–23.

# 3 The coming of convergence journalism

## Executive summary

This chapter traces the evolution of multiple or convergence journalism at a dozen news organizations in four countries. This form of journalism involves re-using editorial material so that one piece of content appears in print, broadcast and online, and can also be made available for portable devices such as mobile phones. Convergence journalism is attractive because it satisfies consumer demands and lifestyles. It also protects an organization's journalistic franchise in the sense that the multiple news format allows wider coverage of an area and permits cross-marketing of a single product. The key unresolved debate concerns whether it should be done to cut costs – multiple-journalism can mean increased productivity – or whether it produces better journalism in the sense that stories can receive the most appropriate treatment. The examples in this chapter show that organizations embraced multiple-journalism for a variety of reasons. Those reasons are connected with the perceptions and background of the people making the decisions. Journalists believe quality must be maintained and call for this to remain the paramount consideration in any change, while managers see the financial benefits of having staff expand their expertise in many formats. Topics covered in this chapter include:

- factors influencing multiple-journalism
- America's first convergence company
- multiple-journalism elsewhere in the USA
- convergence in Hong Kong and Singapore
- changes in Australian newsrooms

❑ multi-media television coverage
❑ opposing views of multiple-journalism.

Editorial managers at media organizations in western Europe, Asia and the USA are investing in multiple-journalism because of the obvious economic advantages. It helps protect newspapers' advertising revenues from competitors and it has the potential to reduce costs through increased productivity. It also has the potential to revolutionize journalism in the sense that reporters have the opportunity to tell stories in the most appropriate form for that story. If a story needs to be told visually, convergence journalism allows newspaper reporters to tell it with sound and vision. At its simplest level, convergence journalism involves re-purposing material so that one piece of content appears in several forms. Thus a story is written perhaps initially for online, then re-cast in broadcast form and later re-written to appear in print, along with any related images. Most commonly, the process evolves at large capital-city newspapers because they have the most staff – typically many times more than the number of journalists at a broadcast or online service. A senior editorial manager decides on the level of multi-media coverage a story deserves. Depending on the level, a reporter produces a Web version plus radio and sometimes television stories, followed by a long print piece. Technology is available to make the story available on mobile devices such as telephones and hand-held peripherals, and may even extend to digital ink systems such as the e-book and e-magazine. Andrew Nachison, director of the Media Center at the American Press Institute, defined convergence as the 'strategic, operational and cultural union of print, audio, video and interactive digital media organizations'. He emphasized that convergence was not defined by any platform and focused on co-operation (Nachison, 2001).

Many editorial managers find the economic argument for this form of journalism attractive. These managers view staff not as journalists but as 'content providers' and perceive convergence as a way of increasing productivity without a similar rise in salaries. Another less overtly economic argument regards journalists as news reporters rather than newspaper reporters – that is, their job is to cover news and to tell the story in the most appropriate medium. This book proceeds from the latter position. New media commentator Steve Outing suggested the Internet 'tech-wreck' in 2000 would help news companies because it would force them to deal with the integration of old and new media. 'The modern news organization clearly can no longer afford to focus solely on its legacy platform – whether print, TV, or radio ... The efficient news organization serves all these media platforms equally well. It doesn't make sense to have one organization serve one set of users and another organization the others' (Outing, 2001). But the over-riding issues must centre on journalistic quality and integrity. Andrew Nachison of the American Press Institute believes that if journalistic values prevail in the move to multiple-journalism, quality will improve. 'The danger seems to lie in making news values subordinate to other business considerations' (Nachison, 2001). Multiple-journalism has profound implications for the practice of journalism and the quality of what news organizations produce. The final chapter discusses this issue and looks at ways to ensure that quality is maintained as change occurs.

This chapter follows the evolution and application of multiple-journalism in four countries and sees this new form of journalism as an extension of information management, in the sense that it shows how journalists control and re-shape their essential raw material: information. The availability of relatively cheap and widespread digital technology makes the changes possible through the availability of an enhanced version of the 'lingua franca' of the Web, hypertext mark-up language (HTML), known as extensible mark-up language (XML). With XML it is possible to convert any form of data into a form suitable for new delivery mechanisms such as wireless application protocol (WAP) via mobile phones, and delivery of data to other hand-held devices. Chapter 6 considers the development of mobile journalism.

## Factors influencing multiple-journalism

Professor James Gentry, dean of the William Allen White School of Journalism and Mass Communications at the University of Kansas, believes several key factors influence whether the adoption of convergence proceeds smoothly or with difficulty. Factors helping 'easy' convergence included a focused leadership, the same owner, a flexible culture, co-location of media outlets, previous relationships between potential partners and no unions. 'Difficult' convergence arises when the organization has different owners, other leadership priorities, multiple managers, lack of relation-ships, inflexible or dissimilar cultures, disparate locations and the presence of unions (James Gentry, email communi-cations with author, June 2001). The availability of appro-priate technology, declining economic conditions and a flex-ible mindset among managers and staff also contribute.

Multiple-journalism became a prime topic of conversation at industry conferences in the early years of the twenty-first cen-tury, and this chapter looks at the early adopters in various parts of the world. In October 2000, Ifra and the World Association of Newspapers (WAN) organized a key confer-ence entitled Beyond the Printed Word. Nearly 500 people from more than 40 countries attended. Publishers at the con-ference endorsed the idea that the news business had gone 'multi-channel'. They noted that, driven by consumer demand for a variety of news sources, an increasing number of newspapers were pursuing multiple-journalism strategies. The publication's content appeared not only on paper and Web sites but also on radio, digital television and mobile devices. The catch phrase has become 'everywhere, all the time'. The vice president for electronic media for the Newspaper Association of America, Randy Bennett, predict-ed newspapers would evolve into 'truly multi-media compa-nies' that would provide a range of services and products to current and new customers. 'Organization structure and processes will change to make newspapers more nimble and responsive' (Bennett, 2000: 1–2). The editor of Norway's

*Aftenposten*, Rolf Lie, said the vision was not about paper and it was not about technology. 'It's about information.' He suggested that today's journalists should say 'I'm not working in a newspaper, I'm working in news' (Lie, 2000: 1). The managing director of new media at Eastern County Newspapers in the UK, Tom Stevenson, who co-chaired the conference in Darmstadt in Germany, said that 'top-notch content' would be the key to a newspaper's success in a multiple-media world. The quality of content would make or break many businesses in the future, he said.

Adi Surpin of the Swiss-based Fantastic Corporation put it more succinctly: 'If you don't have attractive and appealing content, then the game is over [for newspapers]'. One solution was to re-purpose content, and multi-channel journalism was one of the best approaches (Surpin, 2000: 9). Most delegates agreed that for newspapers to succeed in the multiple-media world, their content had to be unique. Noted Bennett: 'While there are clearly major uncertainties that will influence our business, the next several years will bring great opportunities to those newspapers that embrace change and invest to compete in this new environment. The challenge for newspaper companies is to find, recruit and retain technology-savvy personnel' (Bennett, 2000: 4). These changes, while confronting, should increase the need for journalists who are flexible and who understand the potential of technology. The other conference chairperson, Howard Finberg, pointed out that the publishing industry's strength was its staff, and good people would be needed more and more in the 'multi-media, multi-task newsroom' (Finberg, 2000). Noted Ifra's Kerry Northrup: 'Multiple-media is a trend already catching on. Witness the efforts by large newspaper groups around the world to buy and sell properties, enter into alliances and start new initiatives so that they can have co-located print, Web and broadcast outlets. The real question is not how long before it catches on, but rather how long will it take to get good at it' (2000a: 16). Northrup touches on two key issues: the quality of the product and the way that journalists adopt the new tools to tell better stories. Technology makes these changes possible, but journalists, editorial managers and journalism educators will ultimately be responsible for what the public receives.

Many speakers at the World Association of Newspapers (WAN) conference in Hong Kong in June 2001 noted that multi-media newsrooms had moved beyond experiment to become existing models to be researched and pursued. The conference focused on the opportunities the new century was opening up to newspapers while at the same time insisting that quality content should be maintained and developed. A press release announcing the conference noted: 'It is imperative for editors to plan their strategies in advance and to be aware of the customers' needs in the digital society. Cross promotions and alliances with other media strengthen the print industry and prove how online interactivity can be widely used to attract more readers and increase revenue' (World Association of Newspapers, 2001).

The Innovation International media consulting group, based on an online survey of WAN members that attracted 209 responses, reported that three in four editors and managers had said convergence was starting to happen at their organization. Convergence was prospering in many parts of the world, their report said. 'More than 100 companies around the world, according to Innovation's estimates, are currently on their way to full multi-media integration' (Giner, 2001a: 28). While the process sounds simple, the report noted, the 24-hour news cycle and the need for immediacy 'present a challenge for traditional journalists, who are used to one daily deadline'. Just over half of the newspapers employing convergence journalists (51 per cent) reported that it was working well (Stone, 2001: 34–35). The conference heard case studies from news organizations around the world that had embraced convergence, where journalists produced copy for more than one outlet. Takuhiko Tsuruta, president of the *Nihon Keizai Shimbun*, in Japan, predicted that much potential growth was available for businesses built around newspapers. 'Our plan is to become a powerful media organization with newspapers at the core and strengths in Internet, broadcasting and other media. I believe this goal is well within our reach if we can further refine our ability to gather information and make our brand more influential' (Tsuruta, 2001). Ari Valjakka, editor-in-chief of *Turun Sanomat* in Finland, said each year his newsroom produced 9000 broadsheet pages, 900 hours of television programmes, teletext, an Internet version of the newspaper, a telefax newspaper plus information on cable for the City of Turku – all from the same editorial sources. This multi-media approach enabled the organization to reach two in five of the country's population. It also offered job enrichment for journalists, Valjakka said. Training in all areas improved journalists' job opportunities in all media (Valjakka, 2001).

## America's first convergence company

The Tribune company in the USA has been working on mul-

**Figure 3.1** A view of the converged newsroom at CNN Asia–Pacific's headquarters in Hong Kong. Online staff are on the left and television staff on the right. Photograph Stephen Quinn

tiple-journalism longer than any print-based organization in that country, so it is appropriate to discuss it first. A final section outlines CNN's experiences, based on their claim to be the oldest multi-media company. Tribune has been involved in multiple-journalism since the early 1990s. Late in 1997 the *American Journalism Review* commissioned Ken Auletta to write the first in a series of reports on 'the state of the American newspaper'. He chose the Tribune company as the subject. Tribune was the first US media company to embrace new media and convergence. Other companies in western Europe, such as Ari Valjakka's *Turun Sanomat* in Finland, have been involved in convergence for most of the 1990s. Tribune CEO John Madigan said his company's mantra was 'synergy'. 'Each Tribune property sees itself as an information company, not just a newspaper,' Auletta reported. 'Each has a multimedia desk. Each has an online newspaper. Each has a TV broadcast partner or a 24-hour cable news partner' (Auletta, 1998: 30).

In Chicago, the Tribune company has the advantage of owning the other media outlets with which the newspaper works. In other markets, the papers have gone outside the company to build relationships with other organizations. Early in 2000, for the third consecutive year, the Tribune company's peers ranked it first in *Fortune* magazine's list of America's most admired companies. Tribune generated US$6 billion in revenue in 2000 – up from US$2.7 billion in 1997 – and it employs more than 22 000 people. The company made US$1.033 billion in profits in 2000, a 41 per cent increase on the previous year. It operates three divisions: Tribune Broadcasting, Tribune Publishing and Tribune Interactive. The Tribune company reaches almost 80 per cent of US households daily through those divisions. Tribune Broadcasting owns and operates 22 major market TV stations and reaches 80 per cent of US television households when cable and satellite coverage are included. It is the largest TV group not owned by a network. Its super-station, WGN in Chicago, reaches 51 million households outside of the city through cable networks. It has stations in ten of the nation's top 12 markets, and 16 in the country's top 30 markets.

Tribune Publishing is the second-largest American newspaper group in terms of revenues and the third largest in terms of circulation. The company owns 11 major newspapers, including the *Los Angeles Times*, the *Chicago Tribune*, *Newsday* in New York and *The Orlando Sentinel* in Florida. As of mid-2001, Tribune journalists had won 90 Pulitzer prizes.

Tribune Interactive is a network of local and national Web sites that rank among the top 25 news, information and entertainment networks in the USA. They operate in 18 of the top 30 markets and as of mid-2001 the sites attracted about 5 million unique visitors per month, placing Tribune among the top 20 online news and information networks in the country. The company also owns a small part of America Online (AOL). Tribune Regional Programming runs two 24-hour cable news channels – CLTV News in Chicago and Central Florida News 13. The latter is a partnership with Time Warner Communications in Orlando. The company's publishing, online and broadcasting networks allow it to cross-promote products to huge markets (Tribune company Web site, 2001).

Three main forms of multiple-journalism were being discussed in the USA as of mid-2001. These were being tested at the *Chicago Tribune*, the *Orlando Sentinel* and the *Tampa Tribune* (the last two are in Florida). The first two are Tribune companies, while the last is owned by Media General. Each has developed its own way of organizing how news is gathered. Depending on how one defines convergence, this could be seen as more a form of multi-skilling rather than an integrated newsroom. Ifra's Kerry Northrup believes that the way these newspapers conduct their newsgathering depends on the way they organize the allocation of people and resources and the way they talk to each other internally. This directly influences the form that the newsgathering takes. He suggests that each of the three publications has adopted a different form of interaction. The *Chicago Tribune* uses what he calls the 'negotiation model'. All of the various newsrooms – newspaper, online, television and radio – remain separate and autonomous, despite the fact that a television station sits in the middle of the print newsroom. The paper created a multi-media desk and established the position of multi-media editor to act as liaison between the different news operations. When the television operation wants a story initiated by the newspaper, it asks the multi-media desk. This desk acts as a go-between. For example, it might negotiate with the newspaper managers about how much of the story can be used, and whether the reporters involved are available for a talkback interview on television. The multi-media desk remains 'the primary vehicle for interaction'. The key to the allocation of resources is a process of negotiation.

The *Orlando Sentinel* uses what Northrup calls the 'co-ordination model'. The various newsrooms remain distinct but instead of a multi-media liaison desk, Orlando created the Starship concept. All its media-specific managers sit together so that they can talk to each another and hopefully work together. 'By sitting in proximity rather than in their own isolated offices, they hear one another on the phone or talking to reporters. TV hears when the newspaper gets a new story. So early on the two managers can be discussing how they might share the resulting news content.' When a reporter submits a story, for example, the television manager knows about it almost as soon as the newspaper manager because they are sitting together. Decisions are made and resources allocated by allowing people to find the best way to work together.

The *Tampa Tribune* uses what Northrup calls the 'co-operation model'. Again, the newsrooms remain distinct, and the organization has a multi-media editor. This editor's job is to launch and manage an involved planning process once he or someone else identifies a story that the different newsrooms can work on together. This method puts the multi-media editor at the centre of the newsgathering operation and requires people to work together with the editor as the lynch pin.

Juan Antonio Giner of the Innovation International media consulting group said no American newspaper group had yet achieved true convergence. He argued they were only part of the way towards a new form of media organization. For Dr Giner, convergence involved an integrated newsroom that worked as a 'news factory' or 'news information pool'. That is, the one newsroom would provide content for all media. Dr Giner concluded that some American newsrooms had managed to co-operate and share resources, but 'co-operation is not convergence'. These papers had not solved two major convergence challenges: they had not established a fully integrated multi-media editorial system, and their newsrooms continued to work as separate entities with one for print, another for the online edition and a third for the broadcast media. 'Of course, the co-operation works nicely when you sell multi-media advertising packages, or when you do cross-promotion. But this is not convergence, believe me' (Giner, 2001b).

Elsewhere in Florida, the Sarasota *Herald-Tribune* has partnered with Comcast Cable to operate a cable news channel, Six News Now (SNN), which is based in the *Herald-Tribune*'s newsroom. In 1994 a local cable franchise's new manager was looking for joint ventures and the paper decided to join forces to launch a 24-hour cable news channel. It had the encouragement and financial support of The New York Times Company, the *Herald-Tribune*'s owner. Diane McFarlin, then the paper's executive editor, was made director of broadcasting. She had responsibility for installing the TV operation in her newsroom and combining the talents of her print news staff with those of the on-air team she was assembling. Frank Verdel, a respected TV news manager, was appointed general manager in December 1994 and SNN went on air in July 1995. McFarlin said the print and broadcast teams were co-ordinated by editors on a multi-media desk, where assignments were assessed for 'synergistic opportunities'. In 2000 the operation had 160 print staff and 30 broadcast people. Print reporters commonly write voice-over scripts for TV from their news stories. Some print reporters do pieces-to-camera, and a few have regular programme segments. *Herald-Tribune* photographers and SNN videographers often carry each other's tools and share assignments. Collaboration on special projects is common, as is cross-promotion. McFarlin, now the paper's publisher, believes that SNN reaches people who ordinarily do not read the paper and she notes surveys that say it drives readers to the *Herald-Tribune*. The exercise of creating a cable news service also eased the transition to the Web, she said. The key to the whole process was training, McFarlin said, because reporters familiar with one form of journalism were often not confident in another. 'Accept that there will be a steep learning curve, and promote the benefits of change' (Parsons, 2000).

Speakers at another Ifra seminar in October 2000, on the 'Newsroom for a Digital Age', mentioned flexibility as a key factor in helping their newsrooms deal with new and changing demands. Newspaper editors once wanted people to think solely of the printed product as their main source of news and information. Editors now believed the key was to get customers to regard the company as the source of their news, regardless of the medium. Howard Tyner, then editor of the *Chicago Tribune* and later vice-president of the Tribune company, said the business of journalism was really about 'collecting eyeballs' – in other words, getting as many people as possible to regard your organization as the source of their news and information. 'We go where the audience is,' Mr Tyner said. As well as multiple-journalism, the Tribune company is doing this through cross-marketing and promotion among its various media outlets, including the *Chicago Tribune*, the chicagotribune.com, television super-station WGN-TV, all-news local cable channel CLTV and WGN radio (Veseling, 2000: 20). Interestingly, the paper's long-time owner Colonel Robert McCormick chose WGN radio's call letters when the Tribune purchased the radio station in 1924. They stood for 'world's greatest newspaper'. McCormick was unafraid of innovation and embraced it during the 1920s when his fellow publishers lobbied against the upstart new medium. And when television – perceived to be an even greater threat – arrived, McCormick opened his own station, branding it with the same call letters (Lipinski, 2001).

Multiple-journalism has developed most markedly at the *Orlando Sentinel* and the *Tampa Tribune* in Florida. In a report for the American Society of Newspaper Editors' (ASNE) change committee, James Gentry said the *Orlando Sentinel* offered a 'preview of the newspaper of the future'. The most visible symbol of the paper's 'commitment to convergence' was the multi-media desk, or 'bridge', in the centre of the newsroom. From there, six to eight editors co-ordinated the paper's multiple-media coverage. Reporters' desks were arranged around the bridge. Once reporters received an assignment, they wrote stories for the Web or television or radio depending on the assigned level of coverage, and then put together a piece for the newspaper. Video producers and editing equipment were based in the newsroom. The newspaper, Web site and Central Florida TV News 13 were within a few minutes' walk of each other. Gentry described them as a 'campus' where ideas were shared (Gentry, 1999: 4). Links with Channel 13 gave the *Sentinel* the chance to cross-market itself. A consultants' report in 2000 showed that Orlando Sentinel Communications reached 'an enviable' 87 per cent of the total audience via its newspaper, cable television channel and online sites (Nachison, 2001).

John Haile, the *Sentinel*'s editor at the time, acknowledged that initially the decision to travel the convergent route was driven by commercial imperatives – to protect classified advertising considered vulnerable to interactive competition and searchable media. 'I was on an ASNE [American Society of Newspaper Editors] new media panel in Dallas four years ago [in 1995], and I remember answering the question of "why do this?" with two words: "classified advertising",' Haile said. 'That is our largest single source of advertising, and it is the most vulnerable to interactive, searchable media.

If ad[vertising] dollars start dropping, you can bet newsroom budgets will follow. That will dramatically affect our ability to do good journalism' (quoted in Gentry, 1999: 6). In 1998 Tribune papers made 38 per cent of their revenues from classified advertisements (Auletta, 1998: 21–22). Convergence became attractive because of the potential cost savings, the opportunity for cross-fertilization and because it seemed a logical extension of the digital revolution. Haile said that as the *Sentinel* got into new media, it became clear that media would converge, with print, video and interactivity coming together to create a new form of communication. The company had realized that 'eventually everything would have to be in a digital format' (quoted in Gentry, 1999: 4).

At the newsdesk at both papers, editors exchange ideas and assign stories among the various forms of media. The *Sentinel*'s television production manager, Tom Barnes, said Channel 13 alerted the paper about stories. 'A lot happens in the other direction, too,' he said. 'We tend to pass more information from the *Sentinel* to Channel 13.' But almost all of it goes through the bridge. Kevin Spear, a *Sentinel* reporter for more than a decade, is considered one of the paper's most skilled TV journalists. He said he liked working in print and video. 'I deeply believe in this coming together of newspapers and television. I really enjoy TV as a powerful story-telling tool. I'm motivated primarily by having fun with TV. But I also believe it won't be too long until you can't tell the difference between print, TV and online. So it's a good idea to keep your eye on each one right now' (quoted in Gentry, 1999: 5). Journalists at other organizations have come to the same conclusion – television gives them exposure in the community.

A near-new building on the edge of the Hillsborough River in Tampa houses the combined newsrooms of the *Tampa Tribune*, the NBC-affiliate WFLA-TV and a family of Web sites under the TBO.com (Tampa Bay Online) umbrella. The Media General company spent a reported US$40 million on the 120 000-square-foot News Centre, which the *Columbia Journalism Review* later dubbed the 'temple of convergence'.

Work started in July 1998 and staff occupied the site in March 2000. As of mid-2001, Media General owned 25 daily newspapers plus almost 100 weekly papers and 25 television stations. The centre of the newsgathering operation in Tampa is the oval-shaped 'super desk'. This desk, a futuristic pod about a metre and half high at the centre of a main atrium, provides the focus for any multi-media reporting. Staff on the 'super desk' monitor fourteen television sets that stretch across the wall, surrounded by two large clocks, and listen to seven scanners. A multi-media editor acts as the liaison between WFLA, the *Tribune*, and TBO.com. He scrolls through the news budgets of the three organizations, looking for opportunities for converged reporting. 'Budget' is the American term for the list of stories to be covered each day.

Competition is tough in this area of Florida. Tampa Bay is the US's thirteenth largest television market. Media General's competitors include CBS's WTSP-TV, Fox's WTVT-TV, and ABC's WFTS-TV, as well as the *St Petersburg Times* just across the bay. WFLA, the *Tribune*, and TBO.com maintain separate newsrooms and make individual decisions about news coverage. But they hope that sharing the same space will lead to a synaptic intimacy that creates a pervasive, powerful presence. Gil Thelen, the *Tribune*'s executive editor and vice president, was the chairman of the change committee of the American Society of Newspaper Editors (ASNE) in the mid-1990s. That work prepared him for his current role, he said. 'Now I have the big one' (Thelen, 2000). Aly Colón of the Poynter Institute for Media Studies in nearby St Petersburg, said Tampa's approach appeared to be the first attempt to put all three news media in one place at one time. 'They plan intentionally, and strategically, to increase the opportunities for each of them to not only work with, but also work within, each of the other's setting. And they'll be working with each other constantly, every minute of every day.' *Tribune* newspaper reporters appear on, and prepare packages for, WFLA-TV. In turn, WFLA-TV reporters write by-lined stories for the *Tribune*. TBO.com creates deeper news information for readers and viewers. WFLA had 92 staff in 2000 while the paper had 210, so the station takes advantage of the paper's greater resources to produce wider coverage. The Tampa market consists of about 1.5 million households. The *Tribune* sees the benefit of getting wider exposure within, and outside, its own circulation area. Much cross-promotion takes place. Cólon said the WFLA logo and the *Tampa Tribune* flag both had broad recognition and reputations in the Tampa Bay marketplace. Attitudes to how best to cover news vary. The *Tribune*'s managing editor, Donna Reed, maintains the issue is not who came up with the idea that should determine who takes the lead, 'it's who's in the best position to drive the story' (Cólon, 2000).

## Multiple-journalism elsewhere in the USA

Since February 2000, reporters from the *Boston Globe* have appeared on cable channel New England Cable News (NECN) at 12:30 h each week day to offer a series of lifestyle segments. A *Globe* reporter hosts each segment, which runs for 10–12 minutes. Maureen Goggin, assistant to the editor for new media, has a stable of about 30 reporters who appear regularly. All reporters volunteer their time and receive no extra pay. They also received no training in television techniques, though a NECN executive producer spent a week at the *Globe* when the segments started. Goggin noted that younger reporters like appearing on television: 'They realize that this change is not going away. The younger generation of reporters know that they need this experience, or they'll find themselves behind the eight-ball. In this building people are pretty clear that multiple-journalism is the way of the future. When we started this it was an experiment but now it's the norm. The younger reporters realise that they need to adapt and move with the times' (Figure 3.2). In some respects the *Globe*'s arrangements with NECN represent yet another example of 'co-opertition' discussed earlier in the book – the bridging of competition and co-operation where former competitors work together when it suits each party.

**Figure 3.2** The cheerful staff of boston.com, the online edition of the *Boston Globe.* Photograph Stephen Quinn

Goggin noted that each Friday morning, *Globe* reporters appear on radio station WRKO to talk about the major story that will appear in that Sunday's *Globe*. It represents another opportunity to market the Sunday edition. *Globe* journalists also contribute a four- or five-minute segment in NECN's nightly business programme from 18:30 to 19:00 h on week-nights, where reporters and editors talk about the major business news stories that day. Since February 2000, the CBS-affiliate in Boston, Channel 4 (WBZ), has discussed the next day's *Globe* headlines in a short segment during the 23:00–23:30 h news. Initially the newspaper's management worried about giving the rival *Boston Herald* details of major stories but this fear has lessened. (The *Globe* and *Herald* went head to head in a major battle for circulation in early 2001.) On Sundays, *Globe* reporters take part in a public policy pro-gramme called 'News Conference', which screens from 11:30 h until 12:00 h. At 23:30 h sports reporters appear on 'Sports Final'. This show capitalizes on the reputations of

*Globe* sport reporters. On Sundays, the *Globe* publishes a large section on careers and employment called 'Boston Works'. This has migrated to the Web as bostonworks.com and the company planned to launch a television version in May on NECN, under the same name, at 12:30 h. Goggin noted that she spends time 'stroking' journalists' egos to get them to participate in the various segments. 'Building relationships is vital in this business, both with partner organizations and with the *Globe*'s reporters' (personal interview with Maureen Goggin, Boston, 6 April 2001).

Since 1997, reporters at *The Washington Post* have provided televised news updates and analysis from the newspaper's newsroom for a local cable channel, Channel 8. Other relationships have developed with the 'Newshour with Jim Lehrer' on the public Broadcasting Service (PBS), the local NBC affiliate WRC-TV and most recently MSNBC. See details in the 'co-opertition' section in chapter 1. In 1999 the paper launched a special afternoon edition of the washingtonpost.com Web site. It becomes available from 13:00 h and offers stories that broke after the morning newspaper was printed. Often it also contains stories that will be in the next day's newspaper. Analyst Michael Getler noted that the strategy was simple. *The Post*, along with other newspapers, was reacting to the new world of competition represented by cable television and the World Wide Web. 'Wherever people get their news – in print or online – they should get it from *The Post*, or whatever their main newspaper is. Wherever the advertising dollars, especially classified advertising, wind up *The Post* needs to have a print and electronic receptacle to receive it' (Getler, 2000).

As convergence became more ingrained in Tribune newsrooms, so did the expectation that everyone had to participate. Initially reporters were allowed to choose whether they wanted to appear on TV. Now new recruits had to be comfortable with the idea of being on television. Said *Sentinel* managing editor Jane Healy: 'The standards have slowly evolved to where we just expect it of everyone now' (quoted in Gentry, 1999: 7). Then-editor John Haile said that not everyone at the *Sentinel* had embraced convergence. 'We've had some people leave', he said. 'They said this wasn't for them. Their decision was good for both of us.' But what Haile did point out was the importance for the paper's survival of reaching a wider audience. 'We made it clear that this wasn't a lark – that we had to try to figure out how to change the business, because if we didn't we weren't going to have the resources to finance this operation. If we don't keep finding new audiences, and start losing revenues, then this news organization is going to get crunched' (quoted in Gentry, 1999: 6). Northrup noted that the Tampa model was more demanding on journalists. 'What sets the *Tampa Tribune* model apart from either Chicago or Orlando is that the integration is significantly more enforced.' Journalists were expected to learn new skills and accept reporting responsibilities outside their media specialties. Yet early indications suggested that this approach 'has not generated appreciably more or less workplace unrest than in Chicago or Orlando' (Northrup, personal email to author, 1 July 2001). It should be noted that Florida does not have a strong tradition of union membership.

## Convergence in Hong Kong and Singapore

The same could be said of Hong Kong and Singapore, where plans for multiple-journalism started in 1999 and 2000, respectively, though implementation did not start until some months later. Convergence is not an overnight process. These countries have worked hard to encourage innovation in the population, and journalists there understand and appreciate the potential of technology. The governments of both countries decided in the 1980s to invest in information technology to improve the country's economies. Co-operation is also a feature of Chinese culture compared with western cultures, along with a willingness to bring in expertise. Paul Cheung, chief editor of Ming Pao Newspapers in Hong Kong, noted that parent company Ming Pao Enterprise Corporation had hired five senior journalists or photographers from TVB, Hong

Kong's biggest television news station, to help with the move to multiple-journalism. In Singapore, the country's biggest publisher, Singapore Press Holdings (SPH), hired consultants from Reuters and the BBC to help prepare for multiple-journalism. A high-stakes battle for audience share took place between Singapore's two major media groups, who have each gone down the multi-media path in different directions.

Until late 2000, Singapore had three English-language dailies, published by Singapore Press Holdings (SPH). SPH started two more English-language tabloid dailies for niche markets: *Project Eyeball* launched in August and was aimed at the Internet generation, while *Streats* debuted a month later and focused on commuters. *Streats* published about 230 000 copies a day and *Eyeball* about 200 000. In November the Media Corporation of Singapore (MCS) launched *Today*, a tabloid daily. MCS was previously a broadcaster: two of its seven business units operated five TV and ten radio channels – the bulk of Singapore's broadcasting. MCS put up 49.9 per cent of the US$12 million for *Today*, RFP Investments (part of mass rapid transit operators SMRT Corporation) 30.2 per cent and Yellow Pages 19.9 per cent. About the same time, SPH decided to take on MCS head-to-head and announced it would launch two television channels, to open in mid-2001. The SPH English-language channel is called TV Works. Channel U is its Chinese-language counterpart (Singapore Press Holdings, 2000). SPH trained many of its print journalists to supply the content for the news and current affairs programmes scheduled to screen on the channels. The company is due to move to a purpose-built site to house both television and newspaper production late in 2001. In May 2001 SPH published ten dailies: five in English, three in Chinese, and one each in Malay and Tamil but, in June 2001, it announced the closure of *Project Eyeball* because of a slowing economy.

*Ming Pao*'s main opposition is *Apple Daily*, another Chinese-language publication. Chief editor Paul Cheung said competition was intense. The main challenge as the company moved into the multiple-media environment was in keeping all staff up-to-date. With the Internet 'half a year is like three years in the printed world'. 'In the printed world there are many things that everyone has to step up before they can change. Just think about changing your pagination software, you have to get everyone in-line before actual implementation. But not so for dot-com business. Once something comes out your competitor will also try to follow. It is not only a competition among newspapers because everyone is trying to get to the pipe before the others. You are competing against radio, television, etc. The time gap is so short, the investment is so huge and because things are changing so fast, those who stay ahead will come out on top' (quoted in Loh, 2000: 48). Cheung and his staff had several brainstorming sessions and visited newsrooms at *The New York Times*, *USA Today*, the BBC and the *Financial Times*. Senior staff spent one- and two-week attachments in newsrooms. 'We decided the integrated approach was more feasible in Hong Kong. It would be both cost

**Figure 3.3** The newsroom of the online edition of *Ming Pao*, mingpao.com, in Hong Kong. Photograph Stephen Quinn

**Figure 3.4** The newsroom of the print edition of *Ming Pao* in Hong Kong. Photograph Stephen Quinn

effective in terms of saving money and it would prepare us for the future. The integrated newsroom is the newsroom of the future.' *Ming Pao* has 300 editorial staff including 180 reporters, 30 photo-journalists, 60 sub-editors and editors, and 15 news executives. The rest include news assistants and reporters in overseas bureaus. Reporters are assigned to specific desks. These desks cover local news, mainland China, international, business, sport and entertainment. Ming Pao online (http://www.mingpao.com) has 70 staff and produces 12 portals including Ming Pao instant news (http://www.mpinews.com), which is available 24-hours a day and seven days a week. The print edition of *Ming Pao* publishes seven days a week and has a circulation of 100 000 (Cheung, 2001) (Figures 3.3 and 3.4). A study by the Chinese University of Hong Kong rated *Ming Pao* the most credible Chinese-language newspaper in the special administrative region.

## Changes in Australian newsrooms

Only limited forms of multiple-journalism have emerged in Australia because of laws that restrict cross-media ownership. Part 5, division 5 of the Broadcasting Services Act effectively prohibits anyone from controlling more than one commercial radio station or television channel or newspaper in the same licence area. The Hawke–Keating Labor government introduced the Act in 1987. It forbids any one proprietor from owning more than 15 per cent of both a newspaper and television station in any one metropolitan market. Then-treasurer Paul Keating famously said: 'You can either be a prince of print or a queen of the screen'. The US Federal Communications Commission (FCC) similarly restricts any company from owning both a newspaper and a broadcast outlet in the same market – unless the company did so before the rule came into force (as was the case with the Tribune company's ownership of WGN in Chicago), or unless the government finds a public interest in waiving the rule (as it did when Rupert Murdoch was allowed to rescue the ailing *New York Post*).

In the last years of the twentieth century, politicians and media owners have been lobbying to have Australia's cross-media ownership laws changed. Communications minister Richard Alston told a conference on media in the twenty-first century in March 2000 that the Coalition government believed the law was 'flawed', 'ineffective' and 'outdated'. He accused the opposition Labor and the Democrats of refusing to acknowledge the need for change (they have joined forces in the upper house, the Senate, to block law changes). 'Convergence is making a nonsense of cross-media laws' (Alston, 2000: 15). Professor Fred Hilmer, the CEO of one of the country's two major newspaper chains, John Fairfax Ltd, described the cross-media laws as 'ridiculous'. 'We believe that as the rather constraining regulations of the Australian media industry, particularly the prohibitions in terms of cross-media ownership, are relaxed ... that will continue to open new horizons for our company' (AAP, 2000: 25; Gilchrist, 2000: 4). Other Australian leaders and media owners have voiced their opposition to existing cross-media ownership laws. As early as 1995, the chairman of the Press Council, Professor David Flint, pointed out that the arrival of the Internet would produce numerous more sources of news. 'Far from achieving diversity, media regulation has held us back ... The rules on cross-media ownership ... offend a fundamental unwritten requirement of any democracy ... Rather than amending the cross-media rules we should have laws to encourage diversity and pluralism, which encourages new entrants' (Flint, 1995: 2).

Professor Hilmer used a Merrill Lynch investment conference to step up his company's calls for an end to cross-media ownership laws. 'I'd be delighted to see the end of cross-media and would love to have the option of being able to consider combining with a television network. I believe there are a number of areas where you would work together to build brands that are actually quite hard to do when you're in separate entities.' He advocated that the market should be allowed to decide, not government. 'What I'd like to do is have the opportunity to let the market figure out rather than have that opportunity decided in Canberra [the capital]' (quoted in *PANPA Bulletin*, 2001: 75).

Fairfax journalists have a different perspective on multiple-journalism and other changes. In September 2000, they went on strike over pay and conditions – the first time for more than a decade. A key part of the debate was concern that they were being perceived as 'content providers' instead of journalists (Meade, 2000a: 2), plus moves to require journalists to become more like multiple reporters.

The history of Australian journalists' exposure to change, particularly computerized typesetting, has generally been a process whereby technology has been imposed from above. Strikes occurred in the late 1970s and early 1980s because of concerns over health issues and pay (Lloyd, 1985: 277–82).

Introduction of cold metal technology in the early 1980s significantly affected the sub-editors' role. Increased responsibility for the final product, formerly shared with compositors and proof readers, increased stress and job dissatisfaction. Developments in pagination in the 1990s extended sub-editors' tasks and responsibilities. With pagination, subs were responsible for all pre-press newspaper production up to the plate-making stage but salaries had not risen markedly (Reed, 1999: 92).

*The Australian's* Media supplement reported that Hilmer had told staff that reporters needed to take digital audio recorders on assignments and do voice pieces 'the better to keep up with Fairfax's competitors: Yahoo!, News Ltd, the Packer organization and the ABC' (Meade, 2000b: 2). Fairfax controls

**Figure 3.5** Online journalists for News Ltd newspapers in Australia are based at a dedicated site in Sydney that also houses News Interactive staff. Photograph Stephen Quinn

three of Australia's eight biggest papers by circulation and influence. Rupert Murdoch's News Ltd (Figure 3.5) controls the other five. Often the best way to find out what is happening in each camp is to read comments in the rival publications. The Packer organization owns most of the country's biggest-selling magazines. The Australian Broadcasting Corporation (ABC) has a public service approach to broadcasting and has invested heavily in its online product. ABC Online (http://www.abc.net.au) produces one of the country's most respected sites.

All editorial staff at the national news agency, Australian Associated Press (AAP), agreed to use digital audio equipment from the middle of 2000 as part of a productivity and pay-rise agreement negotiated in 1999. Editor-in-chief Tony Vermeer saw the arrangement as an adjunct to the agency's text delivery of news. AAP wanted to be able to offer all forms of reporting in the future. Stories would get the multi-media treatment with moving pictures on an individual basis, he said, with AAP's multi-media editor and individual chiefs of staff helping reporters decide. Eventually reporters would make individual decisions. Selection of stories to cover on camera would be made on a project basis for issues that needed visual treatment, Vermeer said. A small group of AAP journalists with television backgrounds had learned to use digital cameras. They shot and edited in digital form, and stories were sent back to AAP's headquarters in Sydney's CBD via an integrated digital services line. All staff were given a personalized Sony mini-disk digital recorder – the industry standard – and invited to take them home to play with them (personal interview, Sydney, 25 February 2000).

## Multi-media television coverage

Times have changed at CNN as well. Early in 2001, CNN's chief news executive and newsgathering president, Eason Jordan, announced in a memo to staff that CNN would replace its bulky and expensive Beta video systems with compact digital newsgathering gear. This would include digital video cameras and laptop editing systems. 'The days of routinely dispatching three- and four-person reporting teams with cases of bulky equipment are now nearing an end,' Jordan wrote. 'New technologies make it possible to achieve quality results with smaller, cheaper tools. And the splintering of network audiences means that advertising dollars are spread thinner, so dollars must be spent more carefully,' Jordan said. The change in technology was preparation for a changed approach to newsgathering, and an emphasis on multiple-journalism.

Chris Cramer, president of CNN International Networks, noted in an article in *The Guardian* that CNN was devising 'new ways of working' for the more than 1000 journalists who provided content for its 34 different services around the globe. 'Journalists will now acquire the skills and resources to report for all platforms – television, radio and new media. The difference is that we will assign on a daily basis who does what, not who does everything.' Cramer said the move reflected a recognition across the industry that re-invention and change were the only way forward. 'Newspapers are embracing the Web and learning to use video. Television and radio services must develop content for pagers, mobile phones and the Web. To do this, journalists and the systems they work with must be equipped to provide information to these services – fully integrated systems and fully integrated journalists. The days are fast disappearing where newsgatherers work only for TV, radio or interactive.'

Cramer said CNN staff were developing a 'cross-platform' form of writing, a system designed to enable journalists to create content for all known platforms and to store this content, in tagged form, ready for use on platforms and services not yet developed. CNN's 're-invention' of newsgathering was in many ways the result of the availability of cheap digital equipment such as the videophone, which was discussed earlier (Cramer, 2001). In an interview with the *Asian Wall Street Journal*, Cramer said that CNN had invented multi-skilling years earlier when it 'hired a lot of students at very low amounts of dollars'. CNN would not be deploying four-person crews very often, though that could be necessary in war zones or similar situations. 'Generally, we want to employ fewer people faster, and it is a prerequisite that they work across all our services, including the Web.' Cramer outlined CNN's plans in terms of information management. 'We have devised a writing style, which people are being trained in, where you write for different types of platforms. You might migrate the first paragraph onto a pager, the first two paragraphs onto WAP phones, the next three paragraphs into different sorts of text. It might seem incredibly simple and obvious, but in fact nobody has been doing it. So you don't need two or three journalists writing content for different types of outlets, you just need one' (Goldsmith, 2001).

## Opposing views of multiple-journalism

Many news executives believe multiple-journalism is the logical outcome of improved technology and changing audiences. Given the concurrent surge of technology, Northrup is correct in his view that multiple-journalism will be common in less than a decade. It may eventually become the norm at most news organizations. But it is worth considering the views of journalism unions, given the influence that professional bodies can have in the workplace. Gentry points out that unions tend to delay the introduction of multiple-journalism because they do their best to negotiate better conditions on behalf of their members. The Société Nationale de Journalistes (SNJ), the French journalists' union, has about 30 000 members. Its secretary, Francois Boissarie, drew a distinction between what publishers wanted from multiple-journalism and what journalists wanted. 'Publishers are undoubtedly pushing this concept of flexibility,' he said. 'Do journalists want this? It is difficult for me to say.' Boissarie noted that journalists were offered pressured in smaller organizations to have many roles. 'There is less pressure in large editorial departments.' As for learning more about technology, Boissarie called for better training (Boissarie, 2000: 20). In some countries, unions are struggling to attract members. In Australia for example, the journalists' union is said to be at a crossroads. 'Its membership is low and, in some cases, disillusioned, its strength is down, and the opposition from employers is formidable' (Bachelard, 2001: 15).

One of the few dissenting voices in relation to convergence at the 2001 World Association of Newspapers conference came from Walter Keichel, editor of the *Harvard Business Review*. He maintained that news was much more 'medium-specific' than many people believed. Television was mostly about entertainment. 'What was the last big idea or complex story that you came to understand from watching TV,' Keichel asked rhetorically. People did not log onto an online service to 'read' something, as they read a newspaper, he said, but rather to 'do' something – for example, to check sports scores or a stock price or the weather forecast. Keichel was sceptical about convergence because he believed that journalism was 'medium-specific'. 'In my experience, it's a rare print journalist who can be groomed to become an effective on-air "personality", or even as good as a merely average television journalist – maybe one in 20. There are reasons – psychological, intellectual, aesthetic – why one person may go into print and another on air. How many of you, seasoned editors to a person, are as effective or comfortable before a camera as you are with the word-processing program of a computer?' (Keichel, 2001).

Paris-based newspaper consultant Andreas Pfeiffer noted that 'author once, distribute many' was clearly the direction in which newspapers were moving. But he issued a word of caution: 'What has become clear, however, is that implementing this vision is far more challenging than may seem from a safe distance. Setting up system for multi-channel publishing is a complex and costly task. While defining a multi-channel publishing system is relatively easy on the conceptual level, making it work is far more challenging' (Pfeiffer, 2000). Mobile devices were expected to become major distribution media for news in the next decade. They deliver Internet-based data to mobile phones and other hand-held devices. A report conducted for the Finnish Newspaper Association noted that the rapid expansion of mobile phones made news delivery to these devices an important service. As of mid-2001, more than half the population of many western countries had mobile telephones and penetration rates are likely to rise. The report said a key element was machine-readable mark-up languages, like XML, which enabled automatic tailoring of the news to suit different terminals and users, plus wireless application protocol (WAP) (Antikainen *et al.*, 1998: 38–39). Mobile Internet uptake has been slow in countries with small populations and large land masses such as Australia but rapid in parts of the world where many people live in small land areas. In Japan, for example, the national telecommunications company Nippon Telegraph and Telephone was the first in the country to launch mobile Internet access via its DoCoMo service, in February 1999. News was the second most popular subject, after entertainment. As of April 2001, a mere 26 months later, DoCoMo had more than 23 million subscribers (Sinclair, 2001: 5). Chapter 6 discusses mobile delivery of news.

Newsrooms that thrive in the future are going to look and operate much differently than they do today. And journalists will likewise need to work differently. Editorial staff must be willing to embrace the concept of life-long learning. A flexible mindset, or the ability to adjust to change, will be similarly useful. To repeat a key concept from chapter 1: 'If there is one word to describe what is being required more and more in newsrooms as journalism moves into the digital age, it is flexibility. In an industry in which flexibility always has been an important element for success, it now seems to be vital for survival' (Veseling, 2000: 20). The next two chapters consider the tools that help the move to convergence in the newsroom. The next chapter looks at intranets, the Web-based network for linking journalists to allow them to collaborate.

**Figure 3.6** The news desk of the online edition of *The Times* in London. Photograph Stephen Quinn

## How to learn more

1 Read Auletta's *Synergy City* (1998) and Gentry's article on the *Orlando Sentinel* in *Making Change* (1999) to appreciate the background to multiple-journalism in the USA.

2 Subscribe to Ifra's *TrendReport* and *newspaper techniques* to keep abreast of latest changes. See this section in chapters 1 and 2 for details.

3 Attend an Ifra conference on the subject. Monitor their Web site (http://www.ifra.com) for dates.

4 The main American professional journals often contain articles on multiple-journalism. Read the print or online editions of *Columbia Journalism Review* (http://www.cjr. org), *Quill* (http://www.spj.org) and *American Journalism Review* (http://www.editorandpublisher.com).

5 The *Seybold Report on Electronic Publishing* is another excellent source of information, though you will need to subscribe (http://www.seyboldreport.com).

6 If you live in the USA and can afford it, attend one of the 'convergence tours' that the American Press Institute (http://www.americanpressinstitute.org) organizes to multiple-journalism sites in Florida.

## References and further reading

Alston, Richard (2000) 'Why cross-media laws should go'. *The Age*, 29 March, 15.

Antikainen, Hannele, Kostiainen, Kaisa and Sodergard, Caj (1998) 'News content for mobile terminals'. A study for the Finnish Newspaper Association, 13 November 1998.

Auletta, Ken (1998) 'Synergy City'. Part 1 of 'The state of the American newspaper'. *American Journalism Review*, May, 18–35.

Australian Associated Press (2000) 'Hilmer blasts "ridiculous" media regulation'. *The Age*, 12 October, 25.

Bachelard, Michael (2001) 'Union blues', in 'Media lift-out'. *The Australian* 14 June, 15.

Bennett, Randy (2000) 'Horizon watching: seizing new opportunities'. Paper presented to Ifra's 'Beyond the Printed Word conference', Amsterdam, 9–12 October 2000.

Boissarie, Francois (2000) 'Flexibility or mobility: a dilemma to be resolved'. *newspaper techniques*, February, 20.

Cheung, Paul (2001) Personal interview in Hong Kong, 8 June 2001.

Colón, Aly (2000) 'The multimedia newsroom: three organizations aim for convergence in newly designed Tampa headquarters'. *Columbia Journalism Review*, May/June 2000.

Cramer, Chris (2001) 'Journalist, integrate thyself'. *The Guardian*, 2 May 2001.

Finberg, Howard (2000) Finberg is a media industry consultant who founded the Digital Futurist Consultancy (http://www.digital-futurist.com). His paper was entitled 'Classified: Cannibalism or growth impetus', presented at the World Association of Newspapers Conference 'Beyond the Printed Word'. Darmstadt, October 2000.

Flint, David (1995) 'A dangerous dinosaur'. *Australian Press Council News*, August, 2–3.

Gentry, James (1999) 'The *Orlando Sentinel*. Newspaper of the future: integrating print, television and Web'. In *Making Change*, a report for the American Society of Newspaper Editors, April 1999, 3–9. Also email communications, June 2001.

Getler, Michael (2000) 'The new news thing'. *The Washington Post*, 24 December, B6.

Gilchrist, Michelle (2000) 'Media laws in a "time warp"'. *The Australian*, 29 June, 4.

Giner, Juan Antonio (2001a) 'From media companies to "information companies"'. In Innovations in Newspapers: 2001 world report, 28–33.

Giner, Juan Antonio (2001b) Post to http://www.inma.org, 8 March 2001.

Goldsmith, Charles (2001) 'CNN boss finds change necessary for Net age'. *The Asian Wall Street Journal*, 8 February, 6.

Ifra (2001) Trends 2001: Latest trends in multiple media publishing. PDF can be downloaded from http://www.ifra.com, Publications & resources menu option, Books, brochures, download; Trends 2001 booklet.

Itai, Shunji (2000) 'All WAP or what?' Paper presented to Ifra's 'Beyond the Printed Word' conference, Amsterdam, 9–12 October 2000.

Keichel, Walter (2001), 'Co-opetition true and false: an alternative to convergence?'. Presentation to the World Association of Newspapers in Hong Kong, 6 June 2001.

Lie, Rolf (2000). Quoted in The Ifra *TrendReport* 64, 11 October 2000.

Lipinski, Ann Marie (2001) 'Roadmap 2005: National versus regional journalism'. Found at http://www.pewcenter.org.

Lloyd, Clem (1985). *Profession: Journalist. A history of the Australian Journalists' Association*. Sydney: Hale & Ironmonger.

Loh, Peter (2000) 'Credibility of content guides Ming Pao's move to multiple media'. *Newspaper techniques*, December 2000, 46–48.

Meade, Amanda (2000a) Item in 'The diary' in 'Media lift-out'. *The Australian* 14 September, 2.

Meade, Amanda (2000b) Item in 'The diary' in 'Media lift-out'. *The Australian* 24 February, 2.

Morton, John (2000) 'The emergence of convergence'. *American Journalism Review*, January–February, 88.

Nachison, Andrew (2001) 'Good business or good journalism? Lessons from the bleeding edge'. A presentation to the World Editors' Forum, Hong Kong, 5 June 2001. Email communication 12 June 2001.

Northrup, Kerry (2000a) 'The redefined newsroom'. *newspaper techniques* October, 14–16.

Northrup, Kerry (2000b) Personal interview in Melbourne 23 July 2000.

Northrup, Kerry (2000c) 'New skills needed for today's "multiple media" stories'. *Bulletin of the Pacific Area Newspaper Publishers' Association*, November, 32–33.

Northrup, Kerry (2000d) 'Future newsrooms mean re-arranging the furniture'. *Bulletin of the Pacific Area Newspaper Publishers' Association*, April 2000, 55–56.

Northrup, Kerry (2001) Personal email, 1 July 2001.

Outing, Steve (2001) 'Mixing old and new media'. *Editor & Publisher Online*, 31 January 2001.

*PANPA Bulletin* (2001) 'Hilmer defends F2'. May, 75.

Parsons, Allen (2000) 'Experiment with TV leads to cable channel'. Found at http://www.asne.org/kiosk/editor/00.march/parson1.htm.

Pfeiffer, Andreas (2000) 'Emerging opportunities in the expanding media space'. Found at http://www.ifra.com/NewsFeed.nsf on 1 November.

Reed, Rosslyn (1999) 'Celebrities and "soft options": engendering print journalism in the era of hi-tech'. *Australian Journalism Review*, 21 (3), 81–92.

Sinclair, Jenny (2001) 'DoCoMo goes for wireless growth'. *The Age*, 15 May, IT5.

Singapore Press Holdings (2000) Press release found at http://www.sph.com.sg.

Stone, Martha (2001) 'Stepping stones to multi-media journalism'. *Innovations in newspapers*: 2001 world report, 34–39.

'Strategies for a successful future' found at www.pewcenter.org/doingcj/ pubs/roadmap.html (28 May 2001).

Surpin, Adi (2000) Product manager for the Fantastic Corporation. 'Bringing it all together: The multi-media home platform'. Paper presented to the Beyond the Printed World conference, Darmstadt, October 2000.

Thelen, Gil (2000) Presentation to API workshop, Washington, 8 June 2000.

Tribune company Web site (2001) http://www.tribune. com/report2000/ tc2000ar05.html. Found on 30 May 2001.

Tsuruta, Takuhiko (2001) 'The IT revolution and newspaper management'. Presentation to the World Association of Newspapers, 4 June 2001.

Valjakka, Ari (2001) 'Cost-effective multi-media by *Turun Sanomat*'. Presentation to the World Association of Newspapers, 5 June 2001.

Veseling, Brian (2000) 'Flexibility the key in the multi-media world'. *PANPA Bulletin*, November 2000, 20–23.

World Association of Newspapers (2001) Press release found at the WAN Web site (http://www.wan-press.org) 18 May 2001.

# 4 Intranets and knowledge management

## Executive summary

Once issues of mindset and the physical arrangement of the newsroom have been dealt with, technology comes into its own. One of the key ways to apply knowledge management is through teamwork and collaboration – getting people to work together and share ideas. Many brains truly work better than one. But the bigger an organization, the less likely people are able to share ideas. Intranets are powerful tools for linking teams. Often these people work in different parts of the same building within a large organization. Sometimes they work in different parts of the world. Used properly and maintained efficiently, intranets let members of a news organization do better research and 'know what they know'. The latter refers to a key concept of knowledge management that involves getting access to the knowledge inside people's heads. Once more it must be repeated that managers must take the lead and demonstrate their commitment to change through their willingness to embrace technology and, equally importantly, through ensuring that intranets are kept up to date. Topics covered in this chapter include:

❏ what is an intranet?
❏ intranets and collaboration
❏ intranets: catalysts for change
❏ a single source of information
❏ intranets for research
❏ cheaper to distribute electronic documents
❏ intranets save time through convenience

❑ intranets boost morale
❑ anticipating potential problems.

Intranets play a major role in knowledge management because they boost the potential for collaboration among staff, including people in far-flung offices and bureaus. Chapter 2 showed that knowledge management flourishes in an environment in which journalists are encouraged to share ideas and information. Intranets also offer other benefits: they are excellent tools for conducting research and they improve communication and morale among staff. If kept up to date, they provide quick access to volatile data, and they make technology easier for staff to use. All of these factors save time for busy journalists. Along the way intranets provide a return on investment through reducing costs and speeding up people's access to timely data. But the picture is not entirely rosy. To reap the benefits of an intranet, news organizations need to commit to maintaining their currency and preparing for potential problems. This chapter looks at the benefits in the context of knowledge management and also investigates how to deal with potential problems. We'll begin with some definitions and then look at how intranets boost the potential for collaboration.

## What is an intranet?

An intranet is any internal network that operates using the same open delivery mechanisms as the Internet. To install an intranet involves setting up an internal World Wide Web server and placing appropriate software on computers. Any software that uses the Internet's transfer control protocol/ Internet protocol (TCP/IP) would be appropriate. Intranets use the Internet's networking and document distribution standards to serve a company's internal communication needs. As of late 1997, about two-thirds of large American companies had installed some form of intranet and 80 per cent of companies polled by the Meta Group of Stamford in Connecticut realized a positive return-on-investment on their intranet systems (Toner, 1998). Ifra's Kerry Northrup pointed out that intranet technology had absorbed groupware. 'Groupware is the name given in the early 1990s to the class of software popularized by Lotus Notes and intended to allow groups of people to work together more effectively through computers. Until the intranet came along, it was the fastest growing sector of software in the world, including such Notes competitors as Novell's Groupwise, ICL's TeamWare, Microsoft Exchange [and] Collabra's CollabraShare.' IBM subsequently bought Lotus Notes and revised it into the intranet-based Domino product. Netscape purchased CollabraShare and incorporated its functionality into the Communicator series. Microsoft has integrated Exchange into its browser, Internet Explorer. 'Almost every other former groupware product one can name has either died in competition with intranets or has been converted to run on intranets' (Northrup, 1997: 21).

## Intranets and collaboration

One of the key beliefs of knowledge management is the notion that information becomes more valuable when it is shared. The challenging part is organizing effective sharing. Dominic Kelleher, director of global knowledge management communication for management consultants Pricewaterhouse-Coopers, uses a quote from a former head of Hewlett-Packard to make the point. 'If only Hewlett-Packard knew what Hewlett-Packard knows, we'd be three times more productive' (quoted in Lane, 2000). A related and more relevant quote in the context of journalism is one by Arthur C. Clark, the science fiction writer: 'Cave dwellers froze to death on beds of coal. It was all around them, but they couldn't see it, mine it or use it'. Too many news organizations cannot see the resources available to them in the form of their staff. They need to change the culture to encourage collaboration. This could be a difficult task. Former journalist David Walker, now online content director for echoice in Melbourne, noted that journalism has traditionally been a profession that ignored collaboration. 'There's a strong institutional resistance to working together. That has to change' (personal interview, Melbourne, 30 May 2001).

George Brock, managing editor of *The Times* in the UK, agrees that journalists tend to 'squirrel or hoard information' as part of their culture. 'Journalists do this absolutely naturally ... [and] altering journalistic culture in that kind of respect is a very, very large and major piece of work.' Brock said an ideal situation involved having all information stored, accessible and shared, and pointed out the importance of appropriate storage. 'You've got to be very careful about the ways in which certain information is used.' Journalists who gathered huge amounts of data immediately created a number of extra risks compared with their mainstream reporting colleagues, Brock said. 'You've got to be very, very clear-headed about what kind of material they [reporters] are using and you've got to overcome people's prejudices about recording stuff that is sensitive. It will remain sensitive for a very, very long time and is capable of being misused' (personal interview, London, 19 April 2001). Anthony Ridder, chairman of the Knight Ridder newspaper group in the USA, believes newsrooms are difficult places to effect change. 'Newsrooms are, in my experience, reluctant to change the way they do things ... [Journalists] spend much of their professional lives watching establishment figures twist the truth in all kinds of context. Why should they suddenly roll over when you and I say things need to change? It goes against the grain' (Ridder, 2001).

Large news organisations contain plenty of talented people with wide areas of expertise. But the bigger the organization, or the wider its geographical spread, the less likely their expertise can be shared at face-to-face meetings. This particularly applies when staff are in different cities or time zones. But it could also relate to people in the same newsroom if there is no culture of sharing. If the environment exists – that is, if managers generate it – intranets allow people to share knowledge. And searchable databases connected via intranets make it easy to find historical or archived data. For all this to work, editorial managers must encourage and model sharing, and news organizations must embrace a culture where people willingly share information. Too many journalists operate in the opposite culture. They hoard contacts and knowledge, convinced that it is the very exclusivity of these things that makes the journalist valuable. These attitudes, while understandable in a production-era environment, must change in the information age.

## Intranets: catalysts for change

An intranet can act as a catalyst for knowledge sharing. They are designed to increase communications and collaboration between employees, says Ifra's Kerry Northrup. 'They are a bits-and-bytes manifestation of the old saying that "two heads are better than one". The expectation is that innovative ideas and increased productivity will result from a less structured flow of information in and around the organization' (1997: 20–21). In his writings, Northrup cites examples of newspapers using intranets to unleash innovation and initiative. They also undermine traditional layers of authority. 'In every case, the newspaper staff members took advantage of intranet tools to bypass their organisations' traditional information gatekeepers and the established decision-making authorities.' The prospect of intranet-enabled empowerment was sometimes enough 'to spur employee initiative', he said. Northrup quoted Jean-Luc Renaud, technology director at *Le Republicain Lorrain* in Metz, France, who told Ifra's information processing committee how his newspaper's intranet had sprung into life one day in 1996 after a couple of technicians decided that they wanted a better way to co-ordinate their work on computer repairs. 'What they did caught on and now almost everyone uses it – in the newsroom, in the advertising department, everywhere' (quoted in Northrup, 1997: 19). Consultant Alan Burton-Jones pointed out that among western nations, the balance of economic activity was shifting from manufacturing and production of physical goods to information handling and knowledge accumulation, boosted by advances in information technology. 'The commercialisation of IT has largely been responsible to date for this shift to the knowledge economy.' Perceptive companies around the world were responding to these changes by altering the physical design of their environments to force people to meet, all the time using intranets to link people elsewhere.

The pharmaceutical company Pfizer had built a new centre for senior managers and scientists at Walton-on-Thames in the UK, designed to get people to interact with each other. Pfizer designed it from a 'knowledge perspective' so that people would walk between each other's offices and interact 'because they had common meeting spaces'. 'They will meet casually and in an informal setting within the building. It's all based on the concept of improving knowledge transfer and improving decision making, and eventually improving the management of the whole organisation.' This was a way to access tacit knowledge – that held in individuals' heads. Progressive organizations were appointing chief knowledge officers whose task was to integrate knowledge management into the business. It signalled the 'birth' of a new concept of professional knowledge management. The process can save money. In 1993, Dow Chemicals gave a senior manager, Gordon Petrash, the role of evaluating its intellectual assets, including a collection of 29 000 patents. 'The resultant investigation showed that 30 per cent of the patents were rarely if ever used, leading to Dow cutting its patent tax maintenance by US$40 million, and reducing its administrative costs by US$10 million (Burton-Jones, personal interview, Melbourne, 15 March 2000).

Northrup suggests that once an intranet infrastructure is in place and receives management approval, and staff know how to use it, all sorts of benefits arise. For example, messages in a discussion area might start to suggest story ideas, or people might react to story ideas or budgets outlined in the daily news agenda. It is a practical application of Northrup's notion, outlined in chapter 2, that many brains work better than one. 'Two heads are better than one – or in a newsroom's case, 25, 50, 100 or 200 heads probably have something to contribute to newsroom decision-making' (Northrup, 1999). Fahim's large display panels on walls represent another way to involve people in idea creation. Northrup believes that intranets may start the process engineering that the media industry needs, noting that 'calls for a major overhaul of how newspapers think and work are increasingly being sounded by observers both inside and outside the industry who feel the traditionally run print-publishing operation is not flexible or innovative enough to compete successfully in the fast-paced electronic multi-media information age'. These were prescient words, given this was written in 1997 before the evolution of multiple-journalism discussed in the previous chapter. 'For any newspaper trying to tackle the immense task of fundamentally changing the way people work,' he said, 'implementing an intranet could appear to be a relatively simple first step to breaking down organisational walls and weeding out unnecessary middle management' (Northrup, 1997: 20).

Intranets offer immediate answers to the many questions that arise in a newsroom. The defence reporter is about to interview the foreign affairs spokesperson for a country that, though small, is vital for his country's interests. The reporter discovers the spokesperson does not speak English. How does the reporter find someone fluent in their language? The editor of the Newspaper Association of America's *TechNews*, Mark Toner, quoted Kathy Foley who introduced an intranet at *The San Antonio Express-News* in Texas, as saying the intranet enhanced inter-office communication. 'The intranet allows employees to find someone who can speak German at 5 p.m.' Foley, now the paper's assistant managing editor for online news, research and technology, said setting up an intranet could be as simple as dedicating one PC as a server and installing browsers on users' computers. 'Of course, as systems grow, they become more complex, requiring secure servers, firewalls and added security features such as certificate servers.' These issues are discussed at the end of the chapter.

The Knight Ridder chain, the second largest in the USA, has an extensive intranet system. 'An intranet facilitates the exchange of information and knowledge among our newspapers', said Ricardo de La Fuente, Knight Ridder's manager of business information services and technology. 'We're building the highways for that information now' (quoted in Toner, 1998). The Independent Newspaper Group, with headquarters in Ireland, has launched an intranet for sharing stories among daily papers in Britain, Northern Ireland, the Irish Republic, South Africa, New Zealand and Australia. The Independent Media Group works on a policy of editorial 'pooling'. If a story of particular interest to a newspaper breaks in a faraway corner of the world, editors use the intranet and email to locate stories from member publications. 'A group intranet makes the whole process easier to handle and transparent,' said Anne Penketh, the international news editor in London responsible for the site. Photographs and graphics can also be shared. 'Right now we have a group-wide virtual newsroom thanks to the intranet' (Swain, 2001: 20).

Allan Marshall, group technical director of Associated Newspapers in London, publishers of the *Daily Mail*, *Evening Standard* and *Mail on Sunday*, believes organizations tend to function best when staff are able to collaborate on projects and participate fully in things that directly affect them. 'Intranets reward collaboration in that documents and files can be easily shared regardless of the physical location, and encourage participation by opening up the company's workings to comment and discussion.' Intranets provide an easy way to publish documents online. And intranets inherently reward collaboration because they enable people with networked computers to communicate, so employees who do not have the time or opportunity to meet face to face can still collaborate. 'Electronic discussion and news groups, ubiquitous email and networked video-conferencing can all be supported through an intranet, enabling data that wasn't previously accessible to be made available to all' (Marshall, 1997: 33).

In Australia, the country's largest newspaper group, News

Ltd, introduced a major intranet in 1999 in readiness for the Y2K changeover. Group editorial technical manager Peter Cox said each of the company's five major newspapers shared information. 'Each site has its own intranet but they share and cross-link information.' The shared information included training manuals, reference guides, almanacs with useful facts (such as a list of winners of the country's most popular horse race, the Melbourne Cup, and all of the country's governor-generals), phone books and a list of useful Web sites. 'Each site now has hundreds of pages of information. There is no need for all sites to do all this, so [the] Sydney [headquarters] did it well and other sites come to their site to pick it up,' Cox said. 'This means work is not doubled and each division can remain distinct.' News Ltd's multi-media arm, News Interactive, has its own intranet site. Technical development manager at the time, Peter Marks, said the site provided project status, documentation on systems, issue reporting and tracking systems. Development was never a distinct project. Like its News Ltd counterpart, it had grown organically over time. 'It is used for sharing information about current projects, procedure documents and a how-to on source code control,' Marks said. Development staff used it. The issue-tracking system was used constantly and it was the central point for all issues arising in the office and Web sites. 'At News Interactive, the intranet is the business. It's how we do workflow, collaborate, and deliver.'

The intranet at the other major Australian newspaper publisher, John Fairfax Ltd, also facilitates collaboration. Technical services librarian Kimberley Porteous said it was used as a staff directory, with all divisions, titles and contact details provided. 'The directory also lists what languages people can speak at Fairfax, which can be very handy at deadline time when you need someone to translate' (quoted in Murphie, 2000: 21).

# A single source of information

Allied with the notion of collaboration is the use of intranets for research and quick communication. News Ltd's Peter Cox described the corporate intranet as the 'single point of information for the company'. The intranet contained a wide variety of information, ranging from canteen specials and bus timetables to banner advertisements and company training and policy manuals. 'People are made aware of company events and it becomes the single point of information for the company.' Fairfax's Porteous agreed, describing the intranet as the company's most valuable human resources tool. 'It can be hard to communicate in such a large company but the intranet solves that,' she said. 'People who would not normally talk now communicate through the intranet.' The site was also used like an Internet portal. Library staff bookmarked the best sites for staff to use as references – such as dictionaries, federal and state Parliament transcripts in *Hansard* (the official record of debate), currency exchanges and telephone directories. The site offered internal company information such as circulation and readership figures for the major Fairfax newspapers plus editorial, financial and legal information, along with specialty sites for events such as the Sydney Olympics (quoted in Murphie, 2000: 21).

# Intranets for research

In the USA, newspapers of all sizes use intranets to make data available to reporters. Staff at the *Miami Herald* can search databases including campaign contributions, vehicle licences and workers' compensation records. Newark's *Star-Ledger* gives reporters access to a 'virtual library' on its formidable intranet (Boyer, 1999: 49–51). *The Washington* Post has a dedicated information technology department within the newsroom. It employs about 50 people including researchers, librarians and computer support staff. Diane Weeks, the paper's deputy information technology editor, said because reporters did a lot of their own research they used an intranet combined with help from researchers, librarians, two database editors, an application developer and a Web master. 'Everyone in the *Post* newsroom has at their desk high-speed Internet access, the *Post* archives back to 1977, access to 6000 other newspapers, magazines, public records, and wire services through either Dow Jones Interactive or Lexis-Nexis, an intranet, and just within the last 18 months, the output from two database editors who do nothing but bring in databases and make that information available to reporters' (Weeks, 2000).

The Dayton *Daily News* in Ohio created what it called a 'news encyclopaedia' via the intranet. It featured details of major news stories, background information on news topics, information on local buildings, crime, court and police data and biographical files. These files include information on key people in the Dayton area, while the background information on news topics was designed to update reporters on major running stories. The intranet at the *Journal & Constitution* in Atlanta in Georgia offered the publication's stylebook, a calendar of events, a list of news contacts, documents on newsroom policies and training information. At the *Sun-Sentinel* in Florida, technical staff created an intranet that editorial staff used daily. Reporter Diego Bunuel described the intranet as a vast improvement over what he called the 'clunky' Atex system. 'There are quick links to almost anything. It's much easier doing research now. You can find things in seconds compared with using Atex, which took forever to retrieve information. With the intranet, information sources are pooled in one location, making it fast and easy to find what you need.' The intranet was the idea of John Thompson, the paper's associate editor in charge of technology. 'When we started, my vision was to offer remote users a way of getting off Atex and accessing the wires and text archive system and doing their own research.' Then he and his colleagues saw the scope of the project and its potential: 'The intranet revolutionized the newsroom from a research-gathering standpoint'. *Sun-Sentinel* business editor Gail DeGeorge saw the intranet as a newsroom-wide bulletin board that would allow inclusion of style notes and an easy link to the Internet. Ms DeGeorge said she liked the fact that systems editors checked with her and her writers and researchers to find out what sites they use so they can provide links to them. 'Business reporting requires a lot of document research, which means constantly checking out companies on Web sites,' she said. 'The intranet is also great for people in bureau offices. I was a bureau reporter for most of my professional life. One of the frustrating things was that I never knew what was going on in the main office. I always felt out of the loop. The intranet connects everyone to the newsroom' (quoted in Weinstein, 2000: 18).

## Cheaper to distribute electronic documents

Intranets keep data current and manageable, especially with documents that change often, such as telephone books. Kathy Foley at the *San Antonio Express-News* said the phone book was a perfect example of the power of the paper's intranet. 'To print that book used to be an incredibly difficult task because there was no database of who worked where. For the first time, there is a database. That got everybody to realize that this could be the way we do business.' The intranet quickly became the best form of inter-departmental communication, saving at least US$70 000 in printing costs in its first year (quoted in Toner, 1998). Ifra's Northrup noted that a selling point for corporate intranets was the fact they paid for themselves quickly: it is cheaper to distribute electronic documents rather than printing and mailing paper versions. A digital phone book was often faster to access than calls to the operator, and cheaper in countries where telecommunications companies charged businesses for directory assistance. 'But here is a savings that most proponents don't often think about: the cost of an organizational re-engineering consultant. Instead of paying US$20 000 or $200 000 or more to have some outsider come in to explain how a newspaper can flatten its hierarchy, spend as little as US$2000 to set up an intranet server and give everyone free browser and Web-pub-

lishing software. Then watch the hierarchy flatten itself'
(Northrup, 1997: 19). Alan Burton-Jones and other knowledge
management consultants maintain that a flat management
structure boosts the distribution of information and is a boon
to the sharing of ideas.

Marshall observed that a big national newspaper with journalists and offices in many locations across the country and
abroad would spend a small fortune on data communications.
Because intranets used the same protocols and network infrastructure as the Internet (where connections cost the price of
a local call) many communications such as faxes, email and
remote access to computers in different locations would only
cost the price of a local call. This was especially relevant in
countries such as the UK where phone calls were metered by
the minute. Journalists could have access to information from
any location. For example: 'A journalist at a conference in a
remote hotel requires cuttings from the library to complete an
urgent story. Using the hotel phone and modem, he or she can
connect to the company's intranet via the Internet, thus
entailing only local call charges before browsing through the
library's database of cuttings and downloading the relevant
article. He or she could file the completed story as a HTML
document which has been pre-formatted for incoming stories
on the office intranet. Sub-editing should therefore be made
much easier.' Journalists could type in a single query in an
intranet that would return all internal and external information related to that topic. In a well-built system, this could
include internal archive material, a list of possible story contacts from a telephone database and links to outside sources
of information – 'all presented in an organised manner'
(Marshall, 1997: 31). In Sydney, the John Fairfax printing
plant maintains its intranet to store an archive and database
of production processes. Publishing and systems manager
Frank Colls said creating an intranet reduced the need for cir-
culating hard copy, which could frequently become outdated
by the time it was printed and circulated. The intranet placed
the latest information at people's fingertips, and could be easily updated. 'We built an archive database to store informa-

tion from relevant production processes, and that is the core of our intranet' (quoted in Murphie, 2000: 21).

## Intranets save time through convenience

One of the benefits of an intranet for a news organization is the time it saves for busy staff. Journalists thus spend their time doing what they do best – creating content – rather than fighting with technology or waiting on hold. Lisa Peterson, senior information researcher at the *Sun-Sentinel* in Florida, said the paper's intranet brought together all the applications and Web sites that reporters used into a 'single, convenient, easy-to-use location'. 'By using an Internet browser, we were able to use one interface for many applications, making it easier [for reporters] to use.' Mike Meiners, an editorial systems editor at the same paper, said reporters found ease of use the best thing about the intranet, especially for staff in remote places. 'In fact, they [reporters] don't need any technical skills. They simply type their stories into a form, or paste it, and click on the submit button, and it goes directly into the [front-end] system. If there is any breaking news the newroom needs to know about, we can post it right away. Our intranet site is set to automatically refresh every hour' (Weinstein, 2000: 18).

When Queensland Newspapers in Australia moved its Cybergraphic front-end system to a Windows platform it provided a more open environment and paved the way for the creation of an intranet. News Ltd editorial technical manager Peter Cox said Windows met the paper's production needs. But keeping manuals, telephone lists and other documentation up to date was a problem. An intranet solved the problems. All the tools people needed were 'at their fingertips', Cox said. The idea caught on at other major News Ltd divisions in Sydney (the *Daily Telegraph* and *The Australian*), Melbourne (the *Herald-Sun*) and Adelaide (*The Advertiser*). 'Each site has its own intranet but they share and cross-link information,' Cox said (quoted in Murphie, 2000: 20). *Utusan* in the Malaysian capital Kuala Lumpar developed its own system for a virtual newsroom. Every journalist was given a password to access the main Web-site <www.utusan.net.my>. After logging in, journalists could see a variety of options such as their assignment for the day, the duty roster, the short message service (SMS) and Web mail. The range of options depended on their level of access. Photo-journalists also received their assignments the same way. Journalists could access the paper's library and resource centre through the intranet (Ariffin, 2001).

Toner noted that the Knight Ridder newspaper chain in the USA had explored placing all financial systems on its intranet. Staff used Web-browsing software and a central Oracle database to issue or authorize purchase orders or requisitions. 'Senior managers who once drafted local budgets using spreadsheet software and then physically mailed them to corporate headquarters now access Budget Builder, an intranet application that culls live financial figures from a back-end database' (Toner, 1998). At the San Antonio *Express-News*, editors and photographers replaced the paper forms previously used for decades to assign photographs with an intranet. Kathy Foley said it enabled staff to monitor the assignments other editors or reporters made. In Munster in Indiana, Howard Publications expanded its intranet and incorporated editorial tools developed by NewsEngin, the software developer founded by George Landau. Extra software developed by the DeskNet company of New York City provided a link to QuarkXPress. 'For a per-seat cost in the three-figure range – yes, that's *hundreds* of dollars, not thousands or tens of thousands – Howard employees had a full-blown editorial system they could modify themselves' (Toner, 1998). When Peter Marks started with CNN.com Asia in Hong Kong in October 2000 he immediately started building a local intranet to share information. 'It is the default page on every desktop's browser,' he said. Making the intranet available to all journalists produced an efficient way to share information because it was 'something they already know how to use'. Marks, CNN.com Asia's technology director, said he and his staff had built more than 20 tools – using common gateway interface (CGI) Web technology – to do daily tasks such as generating statistics and graphs. 'Things that used to be done manually in Excel we try to automate' (email communication with Marks, 11 and 12 June 2001).

## Intranets boost morale

Andrew Nachison, director of the Media Center at the American Press Institute in Virginia, rightly notes that for journalists to do their job properly in the digital world, they need to be properly equipped and trained (2001). 'There's no return on investment without the investment.' But as well as providing significant opportunities for generating collaboration and maintaining currency, intranets also offer ways to boost non-tangible assets such as morale. Northrup suggests the intranet can become a form of virtual water cooler or coffee machine where employees gather to talk about non-work-related issues such as 'finding a reliable child-care provider or selling a used car'. He recommends that managers help draft guidelines for these morale-boosting activities to ensure the extra traffic does not overload the network. At the *San Antonio Express-News* the distribution department posted information about employee awards and citations on its section of the intranet, along with more practical things such as maps of distribution centres and the ZIP or area codes they served. The paper also installed eight public-access terminals in break rooms and production areas and held training sessions for shift workers and other staff who don't spend their shifts in front of computers. This produced a boost in morale for relatively small outlay (Toner, 1998).

## Anticipating potential problems

Some intranets do not function properly because organizations underestimate the amount of work needed to maintain them. Northrup said the most common reasons for an intranet's failure included a lack of commitment from top-level management, inadequate network infrastructure and an overloaded working environment that did not allow employees time to talk in person or online. 'For newspapers that want to avoid any chance of a bad intranet experience, a much more structured planning and pilot process is appropriate.' Northrup noted that professional organizational consultants usually recommended this approach. The major cost was the time needed to keep information current and to manage the network (Northrup, 1997: 21). Marshall said that introducing any form of information system within a newspaper was 'bound to throw up issues which need plenty of advance warning and careful planning'. Maintenance was vital, he said. Some users generated so much data that the system became swamped and valuable potential information got lost in the process. 'Good search engines are useful in this regard but it doesn't negate the need for continual management and supervision of the network' all of which took time and money. Marshall suggested that some staff experienced 'technology fatigue' and did not update relevant data frequently enough, generating reasons for doing things the 'old way'. An organization used to pushing a lot of paper would find a move to electronic distribution 'difficult'. Marshall also warned that users could distrust a network that 'keeps all their dealings with the company centrally stored on a database' (Marshall, 1997: 34–35).

Toner agrees. Intranets may simplify life for both systems staff and end-users but 'don't think the transition is painless – particularly in an industry long-dependent on numerous arcane proprietary frameworks'. The introduction of an intranet involved discarding old tools and network protocols. 'Finding people to tend intranets poses a challenge equal to the technical issues.' Toner suggested that some papers had managed by re-allocating staff positions and using volunteers to update sections of the intranet. 'Part of the success has been picking the right people,' Kathy Foley said (quoted in Toner, 1998). Marshall warned that putting 'enticing corporate information' online presented the danger that people would spend too much time browsing the network when they should be working. Editorial managers had the same fears with the introduction of the Internet at news organizations. But with time the novelty soon wore off. Besides, if the content is appropriate it helps people do their job better. The benefits far outweigh the negatives.

CNN's Peter Marks believes technology can be used to help people use the intranet more efficiently. Some of the updating of content on CNN Asia's intranet was automated. Where people have to update material by hand, Marks and his team have made the job as easy as possible. 'For example the daily rundown is published using Word 2000's ability to save as html. There are "magic" file names where the editor saves his rundown and it's published on the intranet.' CNN has between three and five 'gatekeepers' who use Dreamweaver, a Web publishing package, to update intranet pages. 'When anyone else wants to update a document they come to us with a new version of a document to go up and it's done on the spot. We don't spend much time updating things. We just use it as a central point for storing documents. I probably tinker with it for ten minutes a day on average' (email communications with Marks, 11 and 12 June 2001). Earl Maucker, the *Sun-Sentinel*'s editor, said that of all the technological changes his organization had made in the editorial area, the intranet was 'by far the most incredible'. The intranet helped the newsroom make a 'relatively smooth' transition to a new front-end system. 'When editors and reporters saw the kinds of applications the intranet site provided, it helped sell the whole thing. It gave them an idea of the potential of these powerful computers.' But Maucker warned that even if staff created the world's best intranet the organization was wasting its time if it did not update it often. 'The key to success is continuous support' (quoted in Weinstein, 2000: 19). The next chapter explores some of the other tools available to journalists to help create knowledge and better content.

## How to learn more

1 If your organization already has an intranet, talk to the people who manage it. Seek their thoughts on how it could be improved and find out more about the knowledge base behind it.

2 If your organization does not have an intranet, talk to your library staff to obtain their thoughts on the best way to organize data for it. Also talk to consultants who specialize in setting up knowledge-based technology in organizations.

3 Read books and articles on intranets and their benefits for organizations. Consult some of the articles in the references below. Two of the best books include *Information Anxiety* by Richard Saul Wurman and *Designing Web Usability: The Practice of Simplicity* by Jakob Nielsen.

4 Visit the site devoted to intranets maintained by the Special Libraries Association (http://www.ibiblio.org/slanews/intranets/index.html) to see examples or demonstrations of good newspaper intranets, such as the *Atlanta Journal and Constitution*'s news research information service or the *Sacromento Bee*'s editorial internet assistant.

5 Visit the sites of the major information providers such as The Dialog Corporation (http://www.dialog.com) and Lexis-Nexis (http://www.lexis-nexis.com) to see how these corporations organize data.

## References and further reading

Ariffin, Kamarul (2001) 'Virtual editorial: Utusan's experience'. A presentation to the World Newspaper Association's annual conference in Hong Kong, 5 June 2001.

Boyer, Tom (1999) 'Playing catch-up'. *American Journalism Review* July/August, 47–51.

Burton-Jones, Alan (1999) *Knowledge Capitalism.* New York: Oxford University Press.

Lane, Alan (2000) 'The age of knowledge frontier or fad?' in *Communication World*, 1 June 2000.

Marshall, Allan (1997) 'Intranets can slash newspaper operating costs'. *PANPA Bulletin*, September, 30–35.

Murphie, Nick (2000) 'Intranets streamline newspaper businesses'. *PANPA Bulletin*, June, 20–21.

Nachison, Andrew (2001) 'Good business or good journalism? Lessons from the bleeding edge'. A presentation to the World Editors' Forum, Hong Kong, 5 June 2001.

Nielsen, Jakob (2000) *Designing Web Usability.* Indianapolis: New Riders.

Northrup, Kerry (1997) 'Newspaper intranets: planning and organization'. *PANPA Bulletin*, October, 19–22.

Northrup, Kerry (1999) Presentation to the Newsroom for a Digital Age conference, 7–8 December 1999, Darmstadt, Germany.

Ridder, Anthony (2001) 'Managing newspapers in challenging times'. Presentation to the World Association of Newspapers in Hong Kong, 4 June 2001.

Swain, Greg (2001) 'Pacific region taps into a rich new news source'. *PANPA Bulletin*, March, 20–21.

Toner, Mark (1998) 'Connecting with Intranets'. *Presstime*, December 1998.

Weeks, Diane (2000) Speech to Lotus breakfast at NEXPO in San Francisco, 17–20 June 2000.

Weinstein, Bob (2000) 'Intranets as an editorial tool'. *PANPA Bulletin*, July, 18–19. Originally published in *Editor and Publisher.*

Wurman, Richard Saul (1989) *Information Anxiety.* Doubleday.

Wurman, Richard Saul (2000) *Information Anxiety 2.* Que.

# 5 New tools for journalists

## Executive summary

This chapter looks at more technology available to information-age journalists. It considers first the NewsGear suite of tools that Ifra's Kerry Northrup believes are most appropriate for reporters. The chapter discusses refined forms of information management such as computer-assisted reporting and geographical information systems, and then explores how databases are changing the way that news organizations operate. It concludes with an exploration of extensible markup language (XML), often described as the building block of convergence. Topics covered in this chapter include:

❑ analysing successful data managers
❑ the Advanced Journalist Technology Project
❑ Newsplex: The newsroom of the future
❑ computer-assisted reporting
❑ geographical information systems
❑ databases for information management
❑ extensible markup language
❑ XML enables convergence journalism.

Several tools and technologies that facilitate better information management and thus better journalism have become available in the past few years. As ever, the key to better journalism in the information age is appropriate and on-going training and provision of relevant tools combined with committed leadership. This chapter begins with a survey that suggests that the more time people spend with technology, the more adept they become at dealing with issues of information overload (discussed in the first chapter). In other words, the best way to cope both with technology and data smog is to learn how to use technology better. The tools thus become your friend, rather than something vague and threatening. Given the importance of leadership, news executives must find time to learn more about the tools they and their staff use. The chapter then introduces a range of journalism technologies that Ifra has assembled and tested, and the Newsplex site established at the University of South Carolina to road test an environment appropriate for the information age. Data management tools such as computer-assisted reporting (CAR) and geographical information systems (GIS) are then discussed, along with the development of databases for storing information. Databases play a major role in the information age because they structure data so that they can be shared and manipulated to produce knowledge. The chapter concludes with a look at extensible markup language (XML) because it is becoming the accepted way to make a single piece of information available in a variety of forms.

## Analysing successful data managers

Early in 2001 *The Next Big Thing* (http://www.tnbt.com), an online magazine, published the results of a survey involving 2296 frequent users of the Web and email. The survey asked them how they dealt with digital information. The results showed that 'information overload' was not an issue for people who had become familiar with technology. The people targeted for the survey were described as 'netizens' – the individuals who spend a lot of time on the Internet – and thus were a specific group rather than a slice of the entire population. While it would be wrong to translate the results to the entire population, the survey does show that familiarity with technology boosts productivity among certain types of individuals. Writer Wendy Cholbi (2001) noted that the majority of the survey participants were 'comfortable handling technology and information flow'. Four in five of the respondents characterized their ability to cope with the news, information and electronic devices they encountered each day as 'better than most' or 'excellent'. These people were also optimistic about technology, with seven in ten looking forward to software upgrades. The individuals who felt most able to cope with news and information handled the greatest amount of it. The respondents who rated themselves most overburdened by data actually managed the least amount of it. Cholbi concluded that information anxiety had 'more to do with people's *ability to manage* information than with the *actual quantity* of data' (my italics). The lesson here was that it really helps to know how to use data-handling tools. A related point that Cholbi did not make concerns the influence of perception or mindset. Theories related to adoption of innovation show that perception influences people's willingness to experiment with and learn about new tools. Everett Rogers, who has written extensively about the adoption of innovation, found that perceptions were vital: 'The receiver's perceptions of the attributes of an innovation, not the attributes as classified by experts or change agents, affect its rate of adoption' (1995: 209).

Cholbi concluded that anybody who understood how to use email effectively and how to navigate through data – a basic form of information management – could ward off 'information anxiety' and handle news 'with the fluency that characterises info-copers' (her term for the people comfortable with technology and information flow). 'Email, still the killer application for personal communication, may be critical in information management, too,' she concluded (Cholbi, 2001). The author has interviewed journalists in six countries who regularly use email. Almost all knew nothing about using simple data management tools such as filters. Indeed, research by Professor Tom Johnson of Boston University shows that journalists' data management skills leave much to be desired (1994: 56). All journalists should attend training courses to learn how to take advantage of the advanced options in common email packages such as Outlook and

Eudora. Ifra's Kerry Northrup maintains the journalist of tomorrow will need to have a 'higher technology IQ' than the journalist of today. They need to understand technology as well as they understand how to write well. 'It's not really that much different than if someone came to you today and said "I don't know how to use a telephone". The telephone is a basic tool of journalism today. We don't consider it high tech or anything. If you don't know how to use a telephone, if you're not comfortable talking on a telephone, then your effectiveness as a journalist is severely diminished.' With time, Northrup concluded, news organizations would naturally recruit journalists who were more 'tech savvy than they were yesterday' (personal interview, Melbourne, 23 July 2000). The final chapter discusses the qualities required of the successful journalist in the information age, and suggests that journalism programmes need to make students more aware of the importance of technology.

## The Advanced Journalist Technology Project

The journalist of the future will have many more tools for doing better journalism. In 1997, Ifra launched its Advanced Journalist Technology Project (AJTP) to investigate what tools were available for journalists working in a multi-media and all-digital environment. The project's manager is Kerry Northrup, executive director of Ifra's Center for Advanced News Operations. Northrup said the project evaluated hundreds of products and technologies each year. 'The most innovative and practical earn the NewsGear designation and are combined into a demonstration suite as a model for news organizations and news technology vendors worldwide.' NewsGear's core is a mobile newsroom in a travel case. It cost about US$10 000 and gave a reporter the tools and capabilities needed for any news scene, including access to colleagues, managers and resources, Northrup said. Evaluations in 2001 focused on Palm-based reporting tools and multi-media newsgathering equipment. Northrup travels the world demonstrating the tools. Details can be found at the Ifra web site, and in the 'How to learn more' section at the end of this chapter. It is a formidable collection of technology.

Elsewhere in the world, other organizations are also designing tools for the twenty-first-century journalist. In Stuttgart, Germany, in May 1999, a young journalist, Ellen Tulickas, produced news reports, complete with pictures, directly to the World Wide Web. It was the premiere of a device called the Web Reporter. Her equipment included a headset with a small monitor in front of the left eye and a digital camera in front of the right. A miniature PC and battery on a belt around her hips powered the equipment. Tulickas wrote her reports with a keyboard strapped to her left wrist. The headset weighed 600 g and the PC and battery 1.3 kg. The Xybernaut Corporation, based in Virginia in the USA and one of the world's leaders in wearable computing, produced the prototype of the Web Reporter. Bernd Wiedmann of Xybernaut's German office said the Web Reporter was the most advanced wearable computer in the world – a 'featherweight computer with all the connectivity of a fully functional networked desktop PC'. Tulickas described the equipment as 'the most efficient companion I've ever had' for doing her work. 'Everything I need for work is on my body. To be completely mobile, all the time online, and to report directly from events was a new and fascinating experience for me.' Tulickas said the device felt strange at first but it 'melted with me and my job'. After about 30 hours online she noticed a change in her outlook. 'I felt like I was thinking faster [and] writing faster, and overall I had the advantage of being part of two realities: The reality where I was physically and the virtual reality of the World Wide Web.' Again, read more about this product in the 'How to learn more' section.

In New York, academics at Columbia University's prestigious Graduate School of Journalism have been testing a prototype of a mobile journalist's workstation since 1997. It consists of a backpack computer linked to goggles with a built-in display that serves as the monitor. Reporters write with a stylus on a laptop that weighs about 2 kg. A Web-based menu is displayed in the goggles to provide the journalist with data about whatever they are looking at. Goggles can cause disorientation, so reporters keep track of their location via a global positioning system (GPS) linked to satellites. The GPS provides accuracy up to a centimetre in open areas, though tracking deteriorates when the reporter passes too close to tall buildings or beneath trees. Professor John Pavlik, director of the journalism school's Center for New Media, said the prototype was developed with the aid of US$120 000 a year in grants from the Office of Naval Research and the National Tele-Immersion Initiative, an organization that promotes the use of computer networking technologies. 'One of the most important principles of journalism is to locate a story in a physical space. We accomplish this by situating the news consumer literally at the story's location,' Professor Pavlik said. Feedback from journalism students had been encouraging, he said, though 'users understandably cite the prototype's weight [about 18 kg] and appearance as drawbacks'. If the entire device could be shrunk to an easily portable size, it could become an important information-gathering tool. It could provide immediate context for reporting, leading to greater accuracy. Factors such as broadband Internet access and developments in wireless application protocol could provide ways to accelerate the device's ability to deliver information. Professor Steven Feiner of the university's department of computer science, who helped design the workstation, said he hoped to make it no larger than a hand-held radio and reduce the cost to about US$150. The device was mostly suited for sending images back to base, he said. Facilities for allowing reporters to write reports in the field were not good enough yet. 'We are especially interested in developing this kind of support, with emphasis on how such a system might be used by journalists in the field to develop stories.' It was all part of the Mobile Augmented Reality Systems (MARS) project aimed at exploring the synergy of two promising fields of user-interface research. Augmented reality, in which three-dimensional displays were used to overlay a synthesized world on top of the real world, combined with mobile computing, in which increasingly small and inexpensive computing devices and wireless networking gave users access to computing facilities while roaming.

Not everyone is happy with these technologies on offer, or at least the way they are marketed. Juan Antonio Giner, of the Innovation International media consulting group, calls them 'fiction' journalism. 'Much of the jealousy that media convergence has aroused in newsrooms is brought about precisely by those who present a comic and childish image of supposed "multi-media journalists" armed with electronic gadgets that require them to have several arms, like oriental gods and goddesses, to be able to write words with one hand, tape audio with another, film video with a third and take photos with a fourth – all of which would be sent by wireless transmission instantaneously through antennas attached to their heads.' He particularly singled out the Xybernaut and Columbia devices for criticism, calling the latter 'pathetic' (Giner, 2001: 33). Giner said he was more interested in keeping alive journalism's 'soul' rather than becoming obsessed with technology. This book suggests that quality journalism and technology are both necessary for success in the twenty-first century. They represent equally important sides of a valuable coin.

Northrup noted that journalists he had interviewed were not keen about 'lumbering' into a meeting or news conference looking like 'Robocop'. In venues where newsgathering was discussed, he said, journalists worried that the tools they were expected to use would increase in number and complexity to the stage that these tools were getting in the way of reporting. 'But journalists also say they like the idea of being connected and online wherever they are, so that they can get information and support whenever they need it.' What is the best compromise? Ifra's Advanced Journalist Technology Project had found that the best low-cost and reliable technology consisted of Palm personal data assistants (PDA) plus a keyboard and a clip-on modem. The Palm's operating system was 'nearly indestructible', Northrup said. 'The key to an effective mobile reporter is communications. Advanced newsgathering technology fails if it does not keep an organization's journalists transparently and reliably connected to one another and to all their news resources regardless of whether they are wandering around the building or out covering a story' (Northrup, 2000: 16–17).

Organizations keen to get staff involved in convergence journalism are supplying their reporters with portable digital cameras and laptops. The news director for CNN.com Asia Pacific, John Beeston, said his organization was on the edge of an 'exciting digital revolution' that had the potential to radically alter newsgathering at media organizations. The development of small and inexpensive digital audio recorders and cameras that were broadcast quality had enormous implications – 'not only for the budgets of news organizations but for the way in which journalists work'. The new equipment gave reporters more flexibility, he said. In April 2001 CNN had sent a reporter to Kalimantan in Indonesia with a digital video camera and laptop. She covered the story by telephone for CNN's international programmes broadcast from Atlanta. She also reported for CNN's regional programmes, wrote news stories and filed pictures for the Web. 'When she returned to Hong Kong she brought back some sensational material, which we produced into enduring features. The small, light equipment enabled her to move around with much more ease than a crew of three people with numerous metal boxes. Consequently we were able to get elements of a story that would have been impossible for a traditional TV news crew' (Beeston, 2001). In Australia, the cash-strapped Special Broadcasting Service (SBS) has been sending people alone into war zones and other action areas with portable equipment to report for its flagship current affairs programme *Dateline*. The issue hit the news because some of the people sent to Eritrea and Afghanistan had not been trained as journalists, though they did have television production experience (Little, 2001: 14–15).

Sometimes a significant news event shortens the time it takes for a technology to become accepted. Research into the diffusion of innovation has tracked the often pronounced time lag between the availability of a technology and the adoption of that technology. Often it takes decades before an innovation becomes accepted and used. But in the case of the videophone, CNN's coverage of the departure of the crew of an American spy plane from China generated interest in a technology that few news organizations had used. This was despite the fact that the technology had been available for several years. CNN reporters used a videophone to transmit live pictures of the departure from Hainan island in March 2001. The videophone is carried in a box about the size of a briefcase. A small dish antenna beams the video via satellite to an earth station linked to the home office. The transmission speed is about twice as fast as a standard telephone modem. The Hainan island images were grainy and jerky, but this event proved a pivotal moment for television news. Few organizations were interested in the videophone because of the poor quality of the images. But in remote locations where traditional transmission facilities are unavailable, the videophone enables reporters to transmit live. After CNN's coup in China the videophone's London-based manufacturer, 7E Communications Ltd, said it had been flooded with orders (Associated Press InfoBeat, 2001). Reporters covering the US-led attacks on Afghanistan in October 2001 used video phones extensively. By then they had become standard equipment for correspondents. Northrup noted a trend among news organizations to supply journalists with portable newsgathering equipment that made reporters more mobile and independent of the newsroom. 'It usually starts with laptop computers, digital still cameras and mobile phones for staying in touch and sending story material back to home base.' But laptops are fragile and poorly trained reporters can put them out of commission by deleting the wrong files. Journalists on the road need a wide variety of connectors and cables. Information-age news organizations need to appoint dedicated editorial technology managers to help reporters equip themselves for the field.

## Newsplex: the newsroom of the future

Journalists also need somewhere to test new tools and ideas. Ifra chose the University of South Carolina at Columbia as the site for its Newsplex, a prototype news centre that will showcase the latest tools and thinking about journalism technology. The Newsplex, which cost US$1.5 million, is run in conjunction with the university's College of Journalism and Mass Communications and is scheduled to open in mid-2002. Its brief is to help journalists understand and master 'innovative storytelling and news presentation techniques emerging from the convergence of print, broadcast and online media. It would be used to educate a new generation of multi-skilled and multi-media-focused journalists' (Northrup, 2001a). Dr Lyn Zoch, director of the university's centre for mass communication research, said one of the Newsplex's objectives was to ensure that journalists had access to the latest and most useful of modern information management tools. 'To meet that objective, the College of Library and Information Science at the University of South Carolina has proposed the establishment of the News Media Library and Information Services Center – a unique research, teaching and service centre in partnership with the Newsplex.' Ifra would also identify journalists to undergo intensive training in multiple-media technologies. Editors and managers would be invited to consider the potential of Newsplex technologies from a supervisor's point of view. How could they obtain the most effective results from their reporters and photographers in the field? 'We envision a long life for the Newsplex's role in kicking today's journalists into the twenty-first century' (Zoch, 2001).

Media facilities architect Saf Fahim of Archronica Architects in New York designed the Newsplex as a model for newspaper publishers to study. The design incorporated the latest thinking about how to create an 'information-intensive media workspace', he said. The blueprints had taken into account 'intelligent building, intelligent systems and intelligent furniture' to create an environment that functioned 'as an actual and virtual site for multimedia experimentation'. The Newsplex catered for the needs of both a collaborative news-handling team and individual journalists, yet saved 20 per cent or more on infrastructure costs over traditional editorial spaces, he said. It also provided a more 'productive and desirable environment' for the modern journalist. Fahim has long maintained that traditional newsrooms cause stress. Research has shown that stress kills creativity, the very thing that newsroom managers seek in their staff (Quinn, 1999: 12). Fahim recalled his tour of American newsrooms between 1992 and 1994. 'There was a lot of friction and a lot of negative energy, very contrary to what you want in a creative environment. Which is what a newspaper, believe it or not, is supposed to be' (quoted in Jackson, 2001: 12).

The lower floor of the Newsplex building would contain the main news activity areas, including the central newsflow deck. The upper floor would house areas designed for individual news research and reporting. The Newsplex brochure describes the facility: 'Throughout this environment convergence journalists will have access to the latest and most useful of modern information-management tools. Dynamically configurable info-panels will provide on-demand displays of news resource and management material. A central desk will co-ordinate cross-media news and editorial knowledge/asset management functions. And a line of specially designed and highly flexible workspaces will support multiple-media news reporting and cross-media news production activities. The entire facility will be laced with wireless and high-speed networking. A state-of-the-art communications suite including mobile and video conferencing will keep the news staff members constantly in touch with one another and with their digital infrastructure. A robust database server farm, able to capture, categorize and retrieve any format of news material and news management information, will sit at the core of that infrastructure. Several complete NewsGear mobile multiple-media journalist technology kits, as assembled annually under Ifra's Advanced Journalist Technology Project, will be available for use outside the facility. Overall, the infrastructure has been devised to allow for easy and efficient adaptation to any newly available technology or workflow as desired for testing and use. All the furniture and spaces are moveable and configurable to allow for dynamic re-organization of the workspace. This capability will be continually used as the Newsplex absorbs and responds to the experiences of its professional and student trainees from one session to the next' (Northrup, 2001b). The aim, Fahim said, was to break down the walls that separated people. 'Why can't a writer sit next to a graphic designer and a photographer? We felt the walls between the tribes had to come down.' Partitioned areas around the edge of the newsroom were designed as studios where teams of people could create multi-media news packages. A screen displayed the status of each group's page or assignment. Anyone in the organization could see the pieces of the puzzle being put together and could offer suggestions. 'You can see how the architecture itself can begin to inform even the people working in the core of the newspaper. The plan is completely open, friendly [and] free-flowing. It provides a pool of ideas' (quoted in Jackson, 2001: 12).

## Computer-assisted reporting

Perhaps a dozen books have been written about computer-assisted reporting (CAR) so this section will not discuss it in detail, except to suggest that CAR's major attraction remains its ability to provide stories that originate off the standard news agenda. If unique and compelling content is to differentiate a quality organization from an also-ran, then news organizations need to invest in ways to generate that unique and compelling content. CAR and geographical information systems (GIS) are formidable ways to generate exclusive content. It is no accident that every year between 1989 and 1998 in the USA, reporters who used computers 'significantly' in gathering and analysing data for their stories won the Pulitzer Prize for investigative or public service journalism (Miller, 1998: 5–7). Yet the ability to put data into a spreadsheet or database package and analyse those data is still rare around the world. Brant Houston, executive director of Investigative Editors and Reporters (IRE), noted that many journalists have been reluctant to get involved in CAR because of computer phobia, maths phobia, and – until the 1990s – the difficulty and expense of learning how to use computers and computer software (1996: 3). Even with improved technology, journalists have not embraced CAR. A survey of CAR trainers in 2000 found that half of the reporters at respondent newspapers did not routinely use the Internet for research. And the trainers estimated that only 10 per cent of reporters used computers for the deep or investigative form of journalism. 'Despite impressive work by some technological pioneers, the news industry overall has been hesitant and, at times, resistant to new technology. From database analysis to electronic publishing, use of the computer in the newsroom is often relegated to the technological elite' (Maier, 2000: 95). Maier concluded that lack of management support was an important obstacle to overcome in getting people to become involved in computer-assisted reporting, though the complexity of the technology remained the over-riding difficulty (2000: 108).

## Geographical information systems

Geographical information systems (GIS) represent an even more sophisticated form of CAR. Professor Tom Johnson of Boston University described GIS as a 'merger of cartography and digital databases, working together under the cover of today's desktop computer'. GIS produces maps and companion statistics that show where things are or where events happened, ranging from specific crime incidents, to demographics, to illustrations of flooding or environmental pollution. 'They can include voting patterns, tax assessment, land use or the prevalence of dogs over cats as pets,' Professor Johnson said. He cited the example of Steve Doig and colleagues at *The Miami Herald* who won a Pulitzer Prize for their coverage of the damage caused by Hurricane Andrew in south Florida in August 1992. Hurricane Andrew was the most expensive natural disaster in US history. It killed more than 40 people and caused damage in excess of US$20 billion. 'Doig employed computerized mapping software – then unknown in newsrooms – to create maps correlating property tax assessment records and plots of the storm track. Doig was able to show his readers that if Hurricane Andrew had made landfall just 20 miles further north, it would have roared through the heart of Miami. Physical damage, and quite possibly the death count, could have more than tripled.'

Doig did not stop there, Johnson said. He put together GIS maps to match geographic-specific wind speeds with building damage reports and found more damage in areas that experienced lower wind speeds. 'Having made the invisible visible thanks to the mapping and database software, Doig and other reporters followed their technological lead with the traditional journalist's tool: reporting. They hit the streets to seek explanations from public administrators, insurance companies and contractors as to how lower hurricane winds could produce more damage than high winds. What the reporters found was a litany of shoddy inspection by public officials.' This won them the Pulitzer Prize. Johnson believes that GIS is becoming another indispensable tool for reporters. The development of faster computers with large, low-cost storage devices and powerful software is driving the spread of GIS. 'Add to that the growing availability of digital maps and data with geographic reference points from public agencies, national government organisations and private enterprise, and the growing cadre of people skilled in applying GIS tools in imaginative ways and you have a revolution in the ways stories can be researched.' Johnson believes that 'intellectually aggressive journalists' could use maps produced by GIS to understand a variety of phenomena and to tell the story. 'A map contains more information than any other two-dimensional form of communication' (Johnson, 2000). In an address to the Association for Education in Journalism and Mass Communication in

August 2000, Anders Gyllenhaal, the executive editor of the *News & Observer* in North Carolina, described GIS as a 'tremendous tool'. It allowed journalists 'to create a whole new explanatory element to our reporting' because mapping software provided a new way to use information (Gyllenhaal, 2000: 17). He is to be congratulated for this insight. Technology gives journalists new possibilities if the journalist can appreciate them. And, of course, journalists need to be given the opportunity to learn, through training. But journalists also need to grasp that opportunity, rather than claim they are too busy to attend training courses.

## Databases for information management

In the same speech Gyllenhaal pointed out the 'vital role' that databases were playing in the information business. Newspapers could be using database software to build useful, searchable databases out of the masses of information they collect each day 'on everything from calendar items to school test scores to taxes and money issues'. Is the paper you work for on top of this tool, he asked? Don Oldham, chief executive officer of Digital Technology International in Utah, USA, said newspapers needed to distinguish between two different kinds of information management needs. 'By recognising these differences, it makes it much easier to select the right type of solution for the two types of requirements.' Oldham said relational databases should be used for information that was published while groupware and flat-file databases were more appropriate for non-publishable information such as contact details for news sources or research notes. 'By effectively integrating the two types of database into a unified system, a publisher will have a powerful database foundation to support both print and electronic publishing, including the management of the process.' Publishers would achieve cost efficiencies not possible through approaches such as 'shoe-horning all types of information into one type of database, or at the other extreme [of] trying to interface together a whole collection of single, application-specific databases'. Oldham said the 'middle ground' of using only two types of database – one for all publishable information and the other for all non-publishable information – would yield the very best results (Oldham, 1998: 18).

Let's consider an example of non-publishable information collected by a reporter who returns from a story. She has been to a meeting at the local town hall, and sits down to write what is asked of her – a 20-cm story for tomorrow's paper. But what happens to all the other materials she collected? At many publications, these documents end up in the rubbish bin or at the bottom of the reporter's filing cabinet, never to see the light of day again. At that meeting the reporter collected copies of the mayor's speech, details of a new zoning proposal by a local company, copies of an amended city budget and plans for a special meeting. She also obtained quotes from several officials and people in the audience at the meeting, along with all their contact details. While chasing a town hall official she discovered that on Tuesday nights he goes to the same bar at the same time, and has done so for the past decade. All of this information is a resource for the newsroom, provided it can be captured. Ifra's Northrup believes that newsrooms need technology to manage all those data. 'We need the database, we need the information management functions to be able to capture all of this stuff. And then we need the systems to be smart enough, so that next time when we pop up with an assignment about a [similar] story we are able to pull [it] up out of our database – all of this knowledge and expertise about how to cover it, and the angles to cover and the people to talk to.' Northrup said serious implementation of knowledge management would produce 'a serious return on investment' and the development of valuable assets in the form of knowledge bases of information. Newspapers typically were not leaders in introducing technologies, he said, but the evolution cycle seemed to be progressing a lot faster than it had in past decades. 'Newspapers are recognizing the increasing importance of being an information-based business rather than just a printing-press-based business' (personal interview, Melbourne, 23 July 2000).

Some news organizations have already come to that realization. In July 2001 the *Boston Globe* started the introduction of NewsEngin software to its 330 reporters. George Landau, president of the NewsEngin company, said the *Globe* would be using a version of SourceTracker as their main knowledge management tool. 'Information sharing will be emphasized as part of the initial training.' Landau said he hoped the paper would provide continuing training after the roll-out so reporters would be further encouraged to take advantage of the system's features, which offered heavy emphasis on personal and communal knowledge management. Apart from the *Globe*, ongoing training was entirely absent in the American newspaper industry, he said. 'This aversion to institutionalized training is perhaps the most common obstacle to getting a room full of journalists to work smarter. You can give them a tool, but unless you follow that up with ongoing training, very few folks will ever make full use of it' (email interview, 22 June 2001).

NewsEngin is an editorial application of IBM's Lotus Notes. This software offers a lot of capabilities but people familiar with it also say that it needs a lot of administration and technical expertise to use it effectively. In June 2001, a leading Spanish media group, Grupo Correo, chose a knowledge management system developed by EidosMedia to manage the content for its cross-media publishing activities. EidosMedia was introduced in the first chapter. One of its main products is Méthode, an advanced knowledge management system. SchlumbergerSema implemented the system under licence from EidosMedia. Gabriella Franzini, general manager of EidosMedia, said Méthode had been designed for managing hundreds of users in a cross-media publishing environment based on extensible markup language (XML). XML is discussed in the next section. Grupo Correo (http://www.grupocorreo.es) is based in Bilbao in Spain. Its activities range from the publication of daily newspapers and magazines to satellite and terrestrial TV broadcasting plus radio, cinema and a number of Web portals.

## Extensible markup language

One of the main tools available for doing convergence journalism is an enhanced version of hypertext markup language (HTML) known as extensible markup language, or XML. It adds invisible labels called 'metatags' that describe the objects contained, for example, on a Web page, so that computers know what they are dealing with. Metatags make it easier to extract information from a site to suit a particular use. It has the potential to become a universal form of data exchange. But XML is complicated and each industry needs to devise electronic schemas that describe common processes for that industry. Reuters launched its version, Reuters NewsML, in October 2000. It could become the news industry standard. This format allowed Reuters to pioneer the packaging and distribution of multiple-media news globally. NewsML enables journalists to produce and assemble stories using video, text, graphics, pictures and audio in any language for any platform. Reuters said NewsML would cut the time needed to assemble, manage and archive news. Reuters is the largest news and television agency in the world, with almost 2000 journalists, photographers and camera operators in 185 bureaus in 153 nations. It produces news in 24 languages (Ifra *Gazette* 2000: 10). Ifra's industry technical standards body formally ratified version 1.0 of the NewsML standard in October 2000 at its meeting in Amsterdam. Most of the world's major news agencies – including Agence France-Presse, BusinessWire, the (UK) Press Association, Reuters, UPI, and Dow Jones' WSJ.com – have already declared their intention to use the new standard. Gabriella Franzini of EidosMedia said the switch to XML had to be made transparent for journalists or it would languish. Current editorial systems offered powerful WYSIWYG ('what you see is what you get') editing functions that made journalists' editing work much easier. 'As soon as a journalist sees an XML editor, the first comparison is made with current systems. This implies that XML tools, in order to be adopted by journalists, will have to show at least the same level of functionality as the proprietary editing tools if not even more' (Franzini, 2001).

Peter Marks, CNN.com Asia's technology director, said CNN used XML for all feeds, provided the partners could cope. 'Most are enthusiastic about it.' Stories generated from CNN's three production centres in Hong Kong, Atlanta and London are distributed across television, the Web, wireless and telephones. Journalists usually write one single first paragraph for all versions of a story. Staff called that paragraph the 'blurb', Marks said, 'and the idea is to try to make it stand on its own'. He noted there was much debate about the topic of writing once for multiple platforms. 'In the end what we decided is that we get the journalist to write two versions, one targeted at a longer read such as the Web, and another targeted at short versions such as SMS [short messages].' The journalist sees none of the XML coding. They use a graphical user interface for story entry, editing, publishing to different indexes and ranking on those indexes. '[But] they do decide what the headline, blurb, body, related stories and related links are,' Marks said. The system, called Newsroom Tools, was built in-house. 'I have worked with other newsroom software such as Vignette [Content Management Server] in the past and [have] been very unhappy with the value for money and engineering of them' (email interview, 18 June 2001).

## XML enables convergence journalism

*Seybold* writers Aimee Beck and Luke Cavanagh noted in early 2001 that awareness of and demand for XML were rising rapidly in the news industry. They predicted the transition to an XML-enabled editorial environment would take years to permeate the entire globe but believed its impact would be similar to the change that the Associated Press's Leafdesk brought to American newspapers in the early 1990s. 'Once papers had a digital wire-photo receiver, electronic pagination suddenly changed from pipedream to obtainable goal. In the same way, once papers get their hands on a system that can process XML-encoded multi-media feeds, they'll be a giant step closer to delivering ... their own multi-media news coverage to consumers' (2001: 15). In other words, XML makes convergence journalism possible. XML should be seen as a set of building blocks rather than a tool. It describes how a wide range of data should appear in a multitude of formats, from data on a portable document assistant (PDA) screen or a mobile phone or a newspaper or magazine. Its predecessor, HyperText Markup Language or HTML, is the standard language used to describe documents on the Web. HTML is called a 'markup' language because the software used to build Web pages includes information embedded in the plain text document of the Web page that tells the browser how it should display that plain text. XML employs the same basic structure as HTML and consists of data inside tags (those less-than and greater-than signs) known as 'metatags'. HTML tells a Web browser how data should look. XML defines a standard for creating standards for information exchange in general. XML places tags on content to describe the content's meaning, independent of the display medium.

Let's say we want to distribute an XML document as a Web page. The most popular technique for translating XML to HTML involves a 'stylesheet' as a template. These stylesheets look something like HTML files, but include special tags that describe where to place the data found in an XML document. An XML Stylesheet Language (XSL) processor combines an XML document – the data – with an XSL stylesheet – the rules for transforming data – and reformats the data for whatever device is nominated. That is, it automatically generates a document in another form. For example, a story written by a journalist for a newspaper page is automatically reformatted so that it fits onto the screen of a personal data assistant. XML allows publishers to 'write once and publish everywhere' (Hall, 2000: 61).

Beck and Cavanagh believe XML standards have 'excellent prospects of lasting for years to come'. This is because 'news producers and aggregators will need a standard way to exchange content derived from and destined for multiple media' (2001: 15). Beck and Cavanagh concluded that a wide range of media companies had become aware of XML's 'utility'. 'Newspaper editorial system suppliers that have been dragging their heels on the XML issue must now catch up, or risk losing out to those that anticipated this change. The future of news will be multi-faceted, with packages delivered ready to use in multiple media and in multiple ways' (2001: 18). That has certainly happened at CNN in Hong Kong. John Beeston, CNN.com Asia's news director for Asia–Pacific, described the Hong Kong centre as a 'crucible' for CNN's move into convergence. His journalists worked to produce material for a variety of outlets. Valuable material that 'costs a great deal to produce' was distributed to television, the Web, telephone and personal data assistants. But he issued a word of warning about technology: 'It's easy for us to become fascinated by the technology and forget the message and the audience. All of this new technology is going to be available to an increasing number of people. The devices we are using can be purchased by the consumer in most electronics stores in Hong Kong.' What then will distinguish one news organization from another? Beeston concluded the key factors were the quality of the information and the speed at which it was delivered. 'The challenge for all publishers and disseminators of information is how to capitalize on the opportunities presented by the digital revolution. It is clear that the audience is becoming more discerning as the choices increase.'

Beeston said people's lives were becoming busier. They could access money through automatic teller machines 24 hours a day, shop in all-night supermarkets and trade stocks online. Consumers expected that products and services should be available on demand. What should news organizations learn from this change, he asked. 'All the technology in the world is of little value without content. If we don't maintain and expand the quality of our content, the new technology has the potential to embarrass us and expose the out-of-date nature of a lot of the material currently being presented as news.' Beeston said it was easy to get seduced by the possibilities of technology. 'But technology only works when it is used to serve the audience. So the key is always knowing the audience and catering for them. We deal with people who are time poor' (Beeston, 2001).

Mobile phones have become popular among busy people. In some western nations, more than half the population have mobile phones. The next chapter considers the possibilities for mobile delivery of news and information as an example of catering for a specific audience. It also looks at ways that mobile devices can and are being used to free reporters from the confines of their desks. In this respect, technology offers major promise for journalism.

## How to learn more

1 Read more about the NewsGear equipment by downloading details at the Ifra site. Type www.ifra.com, click on the Research & Consult option, click on NewsOps, then scroll down to Tomorrow's News to watch the video discussed in this section of chapter 1 to see the tools in context.

2 Read more about Xybernaut's Web reporter (http://www. xybernaut.com/wear/wear_case.htm) at the company web site.

3 Learn more about the mobile journalist's workstation by visiting Columbia University's Web site (http://www.cs. columbia.edu/graphics/projects/mars/mjwSd.html).

4 Read about the Newsplex at the Ifra (http://www. ifra.com) Web site.

5 Visit the Web sites of the National Institute for Computer-assisted Reporting (http://www.nicar.org) and Investigative Reporters and Editors (http://www.ire.org) to learn about CAR. Also read the Houston (1996) and Quinn (2001a,b) books in the references.

6 Visit the Web site of ESRI, the company regarded as the IBM of geographical information systems. ESRI (http://www.esri.com) offers a virtual campus where people can learn about GIS (http://campus.esri.com). Some of the modules are free when they are being developed.

7 Join the JAGIS (journalism and geographical information systems) listserv. It can be found at http://groups. yahoo.com/group/JAGIS-L, though note you need to enrol in Yahoo groups first. Thereafter you control your own account. Visit the JAGIS Web site (http://online. sfsu.edu/~jagis), though note this site has different content to the JAGIS listserv.

8 Plenty of companies offer free tutorials on XML on the Web. For example, the Microsoft Corporation library (http://msdn.microsoft.com/library) offers ten interactive lessons.

9 Read about NewsML at the International Press Telecommunications Council site (http://www.iptc. org).

---

## References and further reading

Associated Press InfoBeat 2 May 2001. Found at http://www. infobeat.com/cgi-bin/WebObjects/IBFrontEnd.woa/ wa/fullStory?article=406873613

Beck, Aimee and Cavanagh, Luke (2001) 'NewsML lays groundwork for next-generation news systems'. *The Seybold Report on Internet Publishing* 5 (6), February, 15–18.

Beeston, John (2001) 'CNN Hong Kong: the digital news room'. Presentation to the World Association of Newspapers in Hong Kong, 5 June 2001. Also personal interview in Hong Kong, 8 June 2001.

Cholbi, Wendy (2001) 'Future so bright, gotta wear shades': introduction to tnbt.com's 'The demise of digital dysfunction' survey. Posted 4 June 2001 at http://www.tnbt.com.

Franzini, Gabriella (2001) Personal interview in Boston, USA, 12 April 2001.

Giner, Juan Antonio (2001) 'From media companies to "information engines"'. In *Innovations in Newspapers: 2001 world report*. Innovation International Media Consulting Group 2001, 28–33.

Gyllenhaal, Anders (2000) 'What's coming? Will we be ready for it?: Equipping journalists for the new communications era'. *Civic Catalyst*, Fall, 16–18.

Hall, Richard (2000) 'Why XML structured text is important for printing and e-publishing'. *PANPA Bulletin*, July, 61–62.

Houston, Brant (1996) *Computer-Assisted Reporting: A Practical Guide*. New York: St Martin's Press.

Ifra *Gazette* (2000) Found at http://www.ifra.com.

Jackson, Sally (2001) 'Convergent views'. In the Media section of *The Australian*, 28 June, 12–13.

Johnson, J.T. 'Tom' (1994) 'Applied cybernetics and its implications for education for journalism'. *Australian Journalism Review*, July–December, 16 (2), 55–66.

Johnson, J.T. (Tom) (2000) 'Wind of change: how a team of *Miami Herald* reporters correlated hurricane wind speeds and insurance damage reports to win a Pulitzer prize'. *The Guardian*, 3 July.

Little, John (2001) 'Handicam honchos' and 'News on a shoestring'. In the Media section of *The Australian*, 7 June, 14–15.

Maier, Scott (2000) 'Digital diffusion in newsrooms: the uneven advance of computer-assisted reporting'. *Newspaper Research Journal*, 21 (2), 95–110.

Miller, Lisa (1998) *Power Journalism: Computer-assisted Reporting*. Fort Worth: Harcourt Brace College Publishers.

Northrup, Kerry (2000) 'News Trek: the next generation'. *The Seybold Report on Internet Publishing* 4 (6), February, 16–22.

Northrup, Kerry (2001a) 'Multi-media convergence and new technologies'. Presentation to the World Association of Newspapers in Hong Kong, 5 June 2001.

Northrup, Kerry (2001b) 'Newsplex: where the futures of journalism and news technology intersect'. A prospectus on the Newsplex published in South Carolina, USA.

Oldham, Don (1998) Information types are the key to database publishing systems'. *PANPA Bulletin*, July, 36–37.

Quinn, Stephen (1999) *The Art of Learning*. Sydney: The University of New South Wales Press.

Quinn, Stephen (2001a) *Digital Sub-editing and Design*. Oxford: Focal Press.

Quinn, Stephen (2001b) *Newsgathering on the Net*, Second edition. Melbourne: Macmillan.

Rogers, Everett (1995) *Diffusion of Innovations*, Fourth edition. New York: The Free Press.

Zoch, Lynn (2001) 'Video in print: preparing for a media convergent workplace'. Presentation to the World Association of Newspapers in Hong Kong, 5 June 2001.

# 6 Mobile journalism

| Executive summary |
| --- |

This chapter discusses two key aspects of mobile technology in the context of journalism. The first looks at tools to help reporters spend more time in the field. The second considers the distribution of content to mobile devices. With the first we introduce the possibility of the 'virtual newsroom' where journalists spend more time in the community and are less bound to their desks. It also means that, potentially, journalists will be able to work more in teams because the technology will perform some of the work needed to synchronize people in the field. In the second scenario, mobile distribution may be one future for the delivery of news and information. This chapter considers the content that could and should be made available on mobile devices. Topics covered in this chapter include:

❑ mobile telephone generations
❑ main transmission technologies
❑ wireless application protocol
❑ DoCoMo's i-mode
❑ open versus closed standards
❑ enabling the virtual newsroom
❑ the virtual newsroom in practice
❑ unique issues for mobile reporting
❑ developing wireless content
❑ the future is still unfolding.

Mobile phones and related devices can transform journalism. This chapter will look first at the possibilities that the virtual newsroom offers. But because of the large number of confusing acronyms and formats used to describe mobile devices, we need to spend some time understanding what these terms mean.

## Mobile telephone generations

Mobile telephony is described in terms of generations. The first generation of mobile phones, which became available in the mid-1980s, were heavy and large compared with the tiny devices people use now. They weighed almost as much as a house brick. These first-generation phones were analogue. Digital devices, commonly called second-generation (2G) phones, started to replace them from the early 1990s. Phones referred to as second-and-a-half generation became available from about the middle of 2001. Third generation phones should be common somewhere between 2002 and 2004. Two competing technologies have been proposed for third-generation (3G) phones – W-CDMA and CDMA2000. These can handle high-speed data, possibly including video or animation, and have some potential applications for journalism. W-CDMA, for wideband code division multiple access, is an open standard. An American company, Qualcomm, owns CDMA2000 and users must pay a royalty. Japan's mobile companies have invested heavily in the former (Ries, 2000: 25). W-CDMA will be available in Australia near the end of 2002. It is developing as the global standard for 3G phones.

## Main transmission technologies

Digital phones use two main transmission technologies, known as GSM (global system for mobile) and GPRS (general packet radio service). Analysts predict that within the first decade of the twenty-first century mobile phone carriers will derive the bulk of their revenue from people seeking data services, such as the Internet, instead of the voice services that account for almost all revenue today (Davidson, 2000:

37). GSM is better suited for voice. GPRS is the better system for obtaining data. GSM phones are based on circuit-switched transmission. When someone wants to surf the Internet, a GSM mobile phone connects to a network. This reserves a connection, normally called a voice channel or a time slot, at a base station. No one else can use the same channel, regardless of whether data is being sent. It would be impossible to be constantly connected with GSM because it would be hugely expensive – calls are charged by time rather than data – and require too much network capacity. With GPRS it is possible to be constantly connected to the Internet and email. Users can connect instantly to any network based on an Internet protocol and through that to the Internet via their mobile phones. They will pay only when using applications and for the volume of data they send. GPRS provides peak data rates of more than 100 kilobits per second – ten times faster than the existing mobile rate of 9.6 kilobits per second – though the reality will probably be slower.

With GPRS, instead of occupying a whole voice channel for the duration of the call, data are sent in small packets. Capacity is needed only when data are being sent or received. If the user wants to send email, it is possible to share a channel with several other users because the content, the data, are broken into packets. GSM users only have access to a channel using a single time slot, which means that the speed is limited to 9.6 or 14.4 kilobits per second, depending on the coding scheme employed. More commonly it is the lower speed. A radio base station provides coverage for a specific area, called a cell. It uses a number of radio channels with a given radio frequency. Each GSM channel is divided into eight repeating time slots. When a conventional voice call is made, the user is allocated a single time slot, say time slot one. No other user can use this time slot or interrupt the call. Information is transmitted every time the time slot is repeated. Information from other users can be sent during time slots two to eight. The fact that GSM can combine information in this manner means that a greater number of calls can be handled per cell. With GPRS, several users can share a time slot. If the user requires more capacity, additional time slots can be allocated. Exactly how much bandwidth will be available in practice depends on three factors: the system, the terminal and network traffic. Technically a GPRS system allows speeds up to 115 kilobits per second but in reality most carriers will aim at about 28 kilobits per second, which is still three times faster than the 9.6 kilobits per second of GSM. GPRS will enable reporters to receive ticker-tape style stockwatch reports, check airline timetables and news updates. They will also be able to access company intranets and the Internet.

## Wireless application protocol

Wireless application protocol (WAP) is another way to access the Internet from a mobile phone. Early versions of WAP available from about 2000 were too slow and consumers reacted badly. WAP does not give users a direct connection to

**Figure 6.1** The exterior of the famous Media Lab at MIT in Boston. Photograph Stephen Quinn

the Internet. For Web content to reach a WAP device, it has to barter access to the Internet with a middle person, a WAP gateway. This translates protocols into a new wireless programming language. 'If the page you're trying to visit is written in a WAP-unfriendly language, you probably can't access it at all. And if you can? Instead of looking at the entire Web page, the content from the page is delivered to you four lines at a time' (Mulligan, 2001: 21). But late in 2000 telecommunications companies experimented successfully with using WAP over GPRS. British Telecom's chief technologist, Peter Cochrane, believes that GPRS could be WAP's saviour. In Australia, a service was launched in November 2000 to help business travellers find the cheapest rates for hotel rooms with their WAP phones. People could search for the best rates and then book the hotel room from a taxi as they drove from the airport (Hellaby, 2000: 23). Similar possibilities are available to mobile journalists.

## DoCoMo's i-mode

In Japan, the national telecommunications giant, NTT, operates DoCoMo, which allows mobile access to the Internet. DoCoMo is Japanese for 'everywhere' but it only applies to that country. DoCoMo represents the biggest single group of mobile Internet users in the world. In May 2001, Japan reached the point where it had more mobile connections (66.8 million) than landlines. Of the 57 million people who accessed the Web – in a population of 126 million – 30 million did so with wireless devices. Many of them were young. The Ministry of Posts and Telecommunications said 90 per cent of people aged between 19 and 29 living in Tokyo owned a mobile phone. Tokyo's population in June 2000 was about 28 million. People used i-mode to send and receive email – subscribers receive an email address that consists of their mobile phone number followed by @docomo.ne.jp – as well as reserving airline tickets, transferring money and receiving newsletters. An i-mode phone operates like a cell phone for voice calls. But by pressing the 'i' button the user can access 'content sites' that NTT operates. The connection to the Internet is maintained for as long as the user likes. Billing is based on data sent and received, not on connection time (Monnier, 2001: 52–53). i-mode runs at about 9.8 kilobits per second. Content providers use a 'compact' subset of HTML, known as cHTML, for creating sites. These are said to be relatively easy to create because of the similarities between the two mark-up languages. WAP and i-mode were incompatible as of early 2001 but DoCoMo's chief executive, Dr Keiji Tachikawa, said DoCoMo was negotiating a new standard that would combine WAP with i-mode (Sinclair, 2001: 5).

## Open versus closed standards

DoCoMo's biggest liability is the fact that it is a closed system. It cannot compete with the open systems that have evolved around the world. For example, about 550 companies around the world, including Microsoft, Palm, Symbian, Nokia, Ericsson, Motorola and Sony, are behind WAP. Open standards are the most likely to survive precisely because no-one owns them. Standards tend to be open because organizations have become suspicious of being locked in to someone else's technology, or because they have spent a lot of money developing a proprietary system and then found that open systems are more appropriate. As Neil Budde, editor and publisher of *The Wall Street Journal Online*, advised: 'Don't invest significant time and money developing custom software for an untested platform' (2001: 7). Bluetooth is another of the important open standards. More than 500 companies – led by mobile phone companies Ericsson and Nokia, and technology firms Toshiba, Intel and IBM – have worked on the Bluetooth standard (http://www.bluetooth.com). It defines how devices should transmit data to each other wirelessly. The main aim was to replace inconvenient cables with a single, short-range radio link. Initial versions operated within about 10 m, but later versions extended the distance to about 30 m. Each device carries a cheap chip – costing about US$5 – that connects them to similarly equipped devices such as note-book computers, printers and personal data assistants. It has evolved into a *de facto* standard because the chips are cheap and use small amounts of power, and because of the lack of international standards in mobile devices.

## Enabling the virtual newsroom

Bluetooth has tremendous potential applications for journalism, especially for teams of reporters or for situations where mobility and time are critical. Reporters can be based not at a central city site but more or less permanently on the road. Not too far into the future, a reporter returning on deadline from covering a breaking news story with several text, audio and video reports will be able to transfer files seamlessly to waiting editors. Bluetooth has the capacity to sense the reporter's return and wirelessly download all the files. Bluetooth could also be set up to synchronize data on a reporter's desktop, calendar, PDA, laptop and mobile telephone. Bluetooth could also help turn a reporter's one phone into a three-in-one phone. At home, the phone would work like a hands-free device, allowing the reporter to roam around the building. When they are on the road, it would function as a mobile phone. And when a Bluetooth phone comes within range of another mobile phone with built-in Bluetooth wireless technology, it would work like a walkie-talkie. Newsroom managers will like this last option because it incurs no telephony fees. Bluetooth would thus allow a team of reporters in the field to use their mobile phones with built-in Bluetooth wireless technology to communicate with each other at no cost. The technology also lets reporters connect a wireless headset to their office or mobile phone, to keep their hands free for other tasks. If nothing it will improve road safety records. Bluetooth would also let journalists transfer documents and exchange electronic business cards at meetings and conferences without any wired connections. Some journalists already exchange electronic business cards with their Palm Pilots. For the historians among us, Bluetooth was named after a Viking king, Harald Bluetooth, who united Denmark and Norway in the tenth century. In the future, Bluetooth may have the capacity to unite journalists into more formidable newsgathering teams.

The Gartner Group believes that wireless local area networks are poised for strong growth and will be one of the key drivers behind the spread of mobile computing. Consultant Andy Woo said a surge in wireless computing and deployment of wireless local area networks would increase sales in portable computers. The personal and desktop computer market had almost reached saturation level in many countries. 'But the advent of wireless computing will create a compelling reason for many PC users to go mobile, and will generate demand at the expense of desktops.' Mobiles would grow to 30 per cent of total computer sales in 2005, up from 18 per cent in 2001, Woo said. 'Information workers could easily establish network connections using a portable computer and a wireless link to share data in conference centres and meeting rooms,' he said. For example, medical staff could receive data on a mobile PC from anywhere in a hospital (Woo, 2001: 40). Connections are based on the IEEE 802.11 standard which is becoming accepted around the world. Macintosh PowerBook and iBook users with built-in Airport aerials and cards can receive permanent Internet access. Data can generally be transferred at 11 000 kilobits per second, good enough to permit file transfer, email and Internet access. Some desktop local area networks are migrating to 100 000 kilobits per second, though it should be noted that wireless LANs have an operational range of about 100 metres and should be only deployed in buildings small enough to accommodate those dimensions (Hellaby 2000: 25).

These tools are available to journalists. Ifra's Kerry Northrup has visited newsrooms around the world and notes that a typical newsroom is one big room or lots of smaller locations where journalists turn up for work. 'They may go out to cover a story but then they have to come back to that location to finish the story because it's the only place where they can input text, where they can do research or make phone calls or whatever.' With recent advances in mobile communications technology a more 'distributed' newsroom was possible, Northrup said. News organizations could have reporters in the community, closer to readers. Journalists could communicate with the newsroom via video-conferencing, short messages (SMS) and email. When that digital environment was established, it would be relatively easy to capture data, which meant that it was possible to apply knowledge management principles to improve journalism. 'It sort of evolves as our working habits change' (personal interview, Melbourne, 23 July 2000).

Media commentator Steve Outing believes that news organizations early in the twenty-first century must publish in multiple-media formats, and must get staff back into their community. News would be delivered via print, the Web, email, portable data assistants (PDAs), mobile phones, electronic books, pagers, Internet radio and broadcast radio and television. 'A newspaper company of the near future will likely distribute its content to all of those except broadcast radio and TV. A television news operation is likely to be distributing to all of those except print. And online news entities are likely to even dabble with print and perhaps broadcast.' A news company in the early part of the new century could not focus simply on its legacy platform, be it print or broadcast or online, Outing said. 'It must begin to train its editors and reporters to produce content for the other media formats. Editors must learn how to craft content packages appropriate to a print edition as well as a PDA edition. Reporters must learn how to write a succinct article summary for mobile phone news subscribers; and how to write a story for a print edition and a companion version for the Web that includes complementary resource material' (Outing, 2000). And news organizations must prepare for major improvements in broadband delivery of data, both via cables and wirelessly.

One major benefit of wireless broadband will be the ability to get more reporters out in the community rather than remaining anchored to their desks because that is where they have their Internet connection, personal computer and landline telephone. Outing believes technology will allow reporters to spend more time out of the office while still staying in touch with editors in the newsroom. 'Broadband wireless will make it easier for reporters to efficiently work outside the office. Wireless modems on laptops and palmtops will make it possible for a court reporter to write a story from the courtroom (or the police station or legislative committee hearing) and transmit it directly to the newsroom.' Advances in palmtop technology were especially significant, Outing said, because these devices could replace laptops as a writing tool. 'Envision a reporter covering a trial and sending bulletins and stories from a Palm Pilot equipped with wireless modem and a fold-out keyboard. Using an "instant messenger" application, reporter and editor can even communicate in real time – without the intrusion that speaking on a mobile phone would create in the courtroom. Palmtop accessories now include digital cameras, so the reporter can transmit photos to the newsroom, too.' Outing recommended Ifra's NewsGear discussed in the previous chapter, though he noted that the technology was still 'a bit crude' for that vision to work seamlessly. 'Wireless access for palm devices remains slow, and palmtop digital cameras don't have the resolution for print reproduction.' Outing also pointed out that the trend towards a virtual newsroom would influence how a newsroom was planned. 'Wireless technology advances will mean that reporters won't need to spend much time in the office. Some reporters, depending on their beats, will be able to get by with a small desk that they use only rarely, or a work area shared with other journalists whose work styles keep them mostly out of the newsroom' (Outing, 2000).

## The virtual newsroom in practice

*Utusan*, a daily paper in the Malaysian capital Kuala Lumpur, provides an example of a virtual newsroom early in the twenty-first century. Noridzan Kamal, senior information technology manager for the parent company Utusan Melayu Berhad, said *Utusan* had developed a newsgathering system called an enterprise portal. Of the 300 editorial staff, only 50 were based in the newsroom. These journalists, along with 15 other people, produced the newspaper: 'We are fully digital in pagination'. The rest of the staff worked remotely or from home. The company paid each reporter's phone bill and a flat-rate fee for an Internet connection. As of mid-2001, reporters connected to the company's servers via 56 Kb modems. *Utusan* invested heavily in a robust system with plenty of back-up servers. Journalists paid for their own computers to use at home but the company organizes financing and can get them more cheaply through buying in bulk. Payments are deducted from each employee's salary. To encourage the uptake of technology, the Malaysian government provides subsidies to people who buy personal computers (email communication, 19 June 2001).

Kamarul Ariffin, chairman of Utusan Melayu Berhad, said individual journalists no longer needed to clock in at the office to get their assignment for the day or the week. 'With the advent of computer technology and the availability of necessary infrastructures in Malaysia, it certainly makes no sense for us to remain loyal to antiquated system of newsgathering and publishing. Habits, however, do die hard and it took us over 12 months to convince the work force that there was an alternative system that would be far more beneficial for them.' Provided the reporter completed their assignment and filed with their editor, there was no need for staff to be physically present at the editorial office. Journalists could access the paper's library and resource centre via the Internet. They could also talk to their editors by telephone or online chatting. If a journalist wanted to send a short message, they could use the SMS button on their terminal. Once a story was ready, the reporter sent it to the newspaper via a template. 'When a story has been transmitted and received at the main editorial office, the editor responsible would view, edit, comment and commit the story to the back-end system' (Ariffin, 2001). Kamal said the paper did not monitor the number of stories that individual reporters submitted. 'But the system will show reporters' productivity on [a] weekly or monthly basis.' *Utusan's* photojournalists also work on the road. They transmit photographs from where they take their images using digital cameras and laptop computers. Ariffin said *Utusan's* virtual editorial project was a work in progress and would be completed by the end of 2002. During the transition period, the company was re-writing manuals and re-training staff 'and above all conditioning ourselves to the modern digital age'. 'We firmly believe that when our project is fully completed, we would be able to make a big saving on time and human power' (Ariffin, 2001).

Scotland's new daily, *business a.m.*, used the fact that it was a start-up to take advantage of newly available technologies for newsgathering. It was the first national newspaper established in Scotland for more than 100 years. The head office is in Edinburgh but remote offices are located in Aberdeen, Glasgow and London. Journalists are also based in the Parliaments at both Westminster (London) and Holyrood (Edinburgh). Mobile reporters with Apple Macintosh PowerBooks write their stories into templates that are emailed to head office. Dr Anthony Jackson, the paper's director of information technology, said because of its template-based input system *business a.m.* had the ability to switch to write to fit. This was a common process in Europe. Dr Jackson said that in continental Europe most journalists typed directly into templates so that length and layout are pre-set. Britain is unique. There, journalists write to an approximate word length and then hand their stories to sub-editors who fit the text into the page layout. 'Technically there is nothing to it for us to switch to writing to fit,' Dr Jackson said, 'but in practice we see it as a gradual cultural shift' (quoted in Shipside, 2001: 21). The issue of cultural change and mindset appears yet again. For more on this, see Chapter 2.

Dr Jackson said reporters' stories from remote offices were usually transferred at 9.6 kilobits per second. That was the maximum available with the current generation of GSM mobile phones and was adequate for raw text files, he said, but 'we're really waiting for the better data rates promised by the next generation of phone services like GPRS'. Photographers needed the faster rate of GPRS to upload pictures; otherwise they had to find an ISDN connection. Reporters had become accustomed to 'hot desking', Dr Jackson said. They could plug their laptop computers into a wide area network at any of the four main offices. They carried their telephone number with them, and breaking news was streamed to the screens of their mobile phones. A technology called VOIP, or voice over Internet protocol, enabled this mobility. Voice traffic no longer travels down a telephone wire in the traditional analogue way as waves. Instead, a computerized microphone inside the telephone mouthpiece digitizes the voice as a person speaks and sends the sound file as small 'packets'. It works the same way as data transmitted over the computer network. VOIP means that the network operates as both the phone exchange and the computer network. Phone calls get routed through the wide area network (WAN) rather than national exchanges, which saves money. 'From a capital expenditure point of view, it was similar to a normal phone system,' Dr Jackson said, 'but the beauty of it is that when it comes to the WAN, you plug your phone into a data point and that's it – you've moved desk and your number, all your speed dials and so on come with you' (quoted in Shipside, 2001: 19–20).

Ifra's Kerry Northrup would like to see all editorial staff equipped with laptops with wireless-network connections, and more reporters in the community. 'I'd want to use communications and collaboration tools to let my staff be out in the community and business districts, where news happens and sources are, rather than concentrated in an arbitrary central location.' Global-positioning systems would allow editors to identify a reporter closest to a breaking story, he said. This would 'unshackle' newsgathering while keeping journalists electronically tethered to the central operation. Ideally he would like to see 'mobile phones for everyone' – even people based at headquarters – 'so that no one is tied down to a desk waiting for a call'. John Van Beekum, a former photographer and systems editor at *The Miami Herald*, maintains that with breaking news, the longer reporters stay at the scene, the fresher the news will be. 'This benefits paper publications by feeding news up to the deadline, and it benefits instant-access media by continually updating the story.' He advocated equipping every news journalist, freelancer or wire-service employee with digital tools regardless of whether they were in the field, the office or online (quoted in Cole, 2001).

## Unique issues for mobile reporting

Mobile reporters working in many locations introduce problems that are not apparent in the traditional or static newsroom, especially when the mobile reporters are working in virtual teams. It is impossible for anyone in the field to have an overview, so the role of the co-ordinating editor back at base becomes increasingly important. These people must be able to communicate quickly and clearly with all team members. In complex situations, reporters should be encouraged to take thorough notes to ensure that events are well documented. This improves the likelihood that others who do similar stories in the future will have a model from which to work, and learn from the early team's mistakes. It saves people from re-inventing the wheel – a too common occurrence at news organizations. Any tools created to help mobile reporters need to make this note-taking task as simple and easy as possible. The tools should also help team members discover what expertise is available, where these people are located and how to contact them. Mobile tools should also make data such as news wires and archives easily accessible. And in a world of increasing data overload, the tools should also help filter unnecessary data. Ideally each reporter should have their own device. But given the fact these tools tend to be expensive – especially in their early versions – they may need to be shared. If so, it should be possible to customize them using bio-technology techniques such as fingerprint recognition. Finally, any mobile tools should be easy to use with fast connection speeds. This means minimum speeds of at least 14.4 Kbits per second for text-based connections.

*The Seybold Bulletin* reported that Geac Publishing Systems and a Swedish start-up, Instant Context Technologies (ICTech), demonstrated new wireless tools for reporters in the field at the Interactive Newspapers Expo in Dallas in Texas in February 2001. Both ran on wireless personal data assistants. Geac unveiled FlashNEWS, a piece of software for the Palm operating system that reporters in the field can use to transmit news copy to their base. With the Palm, reporters use either a keyboard or the Palm's touch-screen Graffiti software to write stories. The keyboard is the better option because Graffiti requires the reporter to learn a new process, which takes time. Geac's Web site said FlashNEWS transmitted data as extensible markup language (XML) email attachments that could be read by any system that accepted the established news industry text format (NITF). 'As other front-end systems evolve they will be able to take advantage of the newly adopted International Press Telecommunications Council (IPTC) news markup language (NML)' (Grinberg, 2001). Details are available at Geac's site (http://www.publishingsystems.geac.com). ICTech's tool, FieldWise, runs on a Pocket PC with the compact edition of Windows, Windows CE. *The Seybold Bulletin* said it was designed for sending and creating assignments, contact information and research information to reporters in the field. It would also search the paper's records for other staff who had done work on the assignment's subject matter, provide that work if possible, and provide contact information for that staff member. As well, it would search predefined external media sources and the newspaper archives for relevant information, based on the task notes provided with the assignment, the report said. 'FieldWise uses its own database of information that is derived from the newspaper's systems. The database can be any standard relational database.' ICTech estimated that the server would cost between US$5000 and US$20 000. The client-side software would run to about US$300 per user (Anonymous, 2001). The FieldWise product was more suited to helping to apply knowledge management processes for mobile reporters. It was designed to help reporters discover what expertise was available about a particular story, where those people were located and how to contact them. Research for the FieldWise product was funded by the Swedish Information Technology Institute, and was based on the application of knowledge management principles to mobile journalism (Fagrell *et al.*, 2000: 8).

## Developing wireless content

This final section may not relate to knowledge management, but it connects with the general theme of mobile communication. New media commentator Steve Outing believes news organizations should devote increased resources to developing wireless content in the twenty-first century. 'With wireless services, there's a built-in micro-transactions infrastructure. So there's a business rationale behind [it]. Wireless content – including news – does not necessarily have to be given away free. Would wireless content take off in a big way in 2001? 'Probably not for most news publishers,' he said. But 2001 was the year to start taking it seriously. DoCoMo showed that money could to be made with i-mode mobile content. Outing said news organizations should also begin planning to publish to portable tablet devices. 'As with wireless content, there's a business rationale for preparing to serve e-reader tablet users. While no revenue model has been determined, by any means, the likely one is that e-reader users will pay to read newspapers and magazines (and newsletters and other documents).' Outing also advised publishers to move their organizations toward serving a perpetual deadline. 'After news is reported by your staff, freelancers or wire services, distribute it to your readers immediately – by whatever media you have at your disposal. Welcome to the new news millennium' (Outing, 2000).

As Outing looks forward, it is also useful to look backwards. Mobile content was at the stage in 2001 that the Internet was about 1994. Then, people described it as slow, clunky and lacking in useful content. Neil Budde, editor and publisher of *The Wall Street Journal Online*, looked at coverage of the Internet in 1994 and concluded that the situation he faced with respect to wireless access and other emerging technologies closely paralleled the development of the conventional Web about 1994. 'When you realize how far the past six or so years have brought the Web, it is much easier to imagine what the first years of this new millennium will hold for still-emerging technologies. If one stops and looks back six years, it's much easier to project forward a half dozen more years. The newspaper in your pocket is not that far off. In fact, today, I read *The New York Times* more often on my wireless Palm than I do in print.' Budde said people 'read' the print newspaper and were 'users' of online offerings. One of the ways to understand this difference was by studying dual subscribers – people who paid for both the print *Wall Street Journal* and for the online version. As of early 2001 this group included almost 150 000 people. Many in this group reported reading the print *Journal* side by side with their computer. They browsed headlines and read a few paragraphs or even the full article. When they found an article that interested them, some found the same article online. 'The reason? They want to print out a clean version of the article to save or read later. They want to email a copy of the article to a friend or share a printed copy. They might even save a copy on their hard drive' (Budde, 2001: 7). These are examples of knowledge management in action, as well as an indication of one of print's perpetual attractions – the chance to browse and to obtain an overview of what newspaper editors consider important.

What kind of content works on mobiles and what form should it take? Mobiles differ from other media in the sense that they are personal communication tools. Newspapers are often shared and families tend to watch television together. Radio works both ways – some people listen to it alone in their car or room, while others have it playing in common rooms and other shared spaces. But individuals own mobile phones and are likely to want individualized news and entertainment.

The Journalism Research and Development Centre at the University of Tampere in Finland published details of a study it conducted in 2000 for the Finnish Newspaper Association in conjunction with Ifra and the Scandinavian Newspaper Technology Association. At the time Finland had the most mobile phones per head of population in the world, at just over one in two people. (By way of comparison, on 21 June 2001 *The New York Times* said 109 million Americans had mobile phones, about 39 per cent of the population.) The Finnish study concluded that mobile media would be mostly a supplementary information service compared with other media. Interviewees perceived a mobile as mainly a personal device, 'which would seem to support the idea of personalized information services' (Oksman, 2000). The study concentrated on second-generation phones and should be repeated to see if similar results eventuate with third-generation phones. The study suggested that compact and personal data such as weather, traffic and ways to link directly to an emergency service would be most useful. Local news and sport would also be popular, along with timetables, navigation aids such as maps, and details of cultural events such as reviews and listings. Interviewees in the study wanted to choose content 'according to what they think is personally interesting'. A report commissioned by the Finnish Newspaper Association in 1998 concluded accurately that the next few years would bring huge increases in transmission speeds through technologies like GPRS. It advised newspapers to develop multimedia production processes. News for the Web, people's desktops and mobile editions could be produced with the same technology. The key elements to consider were databases and machine-readable mark-up languages such as XML 'which enable automatic tailoring of the news to suit different terminals and users'. The report issued a prescient warning: 'In spite of the automatic conversions, journalists, photographers, editors and other creative personnel will have to consider the various uses of their material from the very outset. This means that a certain amount of metadata – classifications, indexes, weights, abstracts – has to be assigned to the articles before the publishing. Because this alters the work tasks, it will take time to introduce new practices'. It was vital, the report concluded, 'to start this work as soon as possible' (Antikainen *et al.*, 1998: 38). The next chapter offers a process for those organizations that have not yet started.

## The future is still unfolding

In the early 1990s Knight Ridder's Information Design Laboratory in the Rocky Mountains of the USA spent millions on a project called The Tablet. The prototype weighed about 1 kg (two pounds), was A4 size and about 1.5 centimetres thick (half an inch). It retained the metaphor of the newspaper and relied on mobile phone technology to transmit data. Roger Fidler, the laboratory's director, worked on the concept for several years before Knight Ridder pulled the plug in 1995. For anything to replace the newspaper, it has to be better than the current product. The Internet has not killed print publications because papers are portable, cheap, easy to navigate and cater for browsers (what some people call serendipity, the chance to discover something you were not looking for). Neil Budde of *The Wall Street Journal Online* believes the promise of a lightweight, easy-to-read and fast mobile device with a substantial screen remains viable. He noted that Microsoft chairman Bill Gates had devoted much of his speech at that year's Comdex to the Microsoft vision of a computing tablet. 'A company the size of Microsoft has the resources to place bets across a wide range of technologies, and we can't all do the same. A company the size of Microsoft also has its reasons for making its strongest bets in particular technologies – especially those that will foster the continued domination of Windows software.' Budde said more and more bets were being made on moving computing technologies to mobile platforms. 'Much as the development was coalescing around the Web in 1994, development is moving toward the mobile platform today. As a publisher, we have to pay attention to this movement and find the right way to ride this new wave. The newspaper in your pocket is not that far off' (Budde, 2001: 4). The next chapter considers the implications for journalism of this new wave. It looks at the kind of recruit that the information age requires. And it offers a how-to process for moving the industrial-age newsroom into the knowledge-based information age.

## How to learn more

1 Read Web sites about W-CDMA, such as the 3G home page (http://www.3g-generation.com) and the W-CDMA site of The International Engineering Consortium, which includes tutorials (http://www.iec.org/tutorials/wcdma) and a self-marking test.

2 Learn about the various digital transmission standards by monitoring the Web sites of the large mobile manufacturers such as Ericcson (http://www.ericsson.com) and Nokia (http://www.nokia.com). Many mobile journalists recommend the Ericcson 380 series and the Nokia 9210 Communicator. Details can be found at the respective company's Web sites.

3 The Mobile Media Japan site (http://www.mobilemedia-japan.com) offers plenty of information about i-mode and the mobile industry in that country. Similarly, the online site of *J@pan Inc* magazine (http://www.japaninc.com) has useful information about the Internet in Japan.

4 Read about wireless application protocol at this site: http://www.wap.com.

5 Steve Outing's columns in the online edition of *Editor & Publisher* (http://www.editorandpublisher.com) are a must read to keep yourself informed about new media developments.

6 Read Roger Fidler's 1997 book *Mediamorphosis: Understanding New Media* to get a clear and lucid explanation of the media's historical evolution.

# References and further reading

Anonymous (2001) 'Field reporters get new gadgets for wireless'. *The Seybold Bulletin*, 28 February, 6 (21), 4.

Antikainen, Hannele *et al.* (1998) 'News content for mobile terminals'. Finnish Newspaper Association, 13 November, 1–41.

Ariffin, Kamarul (2001) 'Virtual editorial: Utusan's experience'. Presentation to the World Association of Newspapers in Hong kong, 5 June 2001.

Budde, Neil (2001) 'Wireless Internet news: another challenge for newspaper publishers'. *Future of Print Media Journal*, Winter, 1–9.

Cole, David (2001) 'The completely electronic workflow'. *Presstime*, February.

Davidson, John (2000) 'Data in mobiles to boost revenue'. *The Australian Financial Review*, 5 April, 37.

Fagrell, Henrik, Forsberg, Kerstin and Sanneblad, Johan (2000) 'FieldWise: a mobile knowledge management architecture'. Viktoria Institute, Sweden, March 2000, 1–11.

Fidler, Roger (1997) *Mediamorphosis: Understanding New Media*. Thousand Oaks, CA: Pine Forge Press.

Grinberg, Bernard (2001) 'Geac FlashNEWS: mobile copy and picture transmission with a PDA'. Found at http://www.publishingsystems.geac.com/default.asp?Page=news_03_09_01. Grinberg is president of Geac Publishing Systems.

Hadfield, Peter (2000) 'Sayonara WAP'. *New Scientist*, 21 October 2000.

Hellaby, David (2000) 'WAP update'. *Road Warrior*, December, 22–23. 'Portable business'. *Road Warrior*, December, 24–27.

Joyce, Daryl (2001) 'Stay out of the GPRS hype trap'. *The Australian*, 20 February, 49.

Meredith, Helen (2000) 'Telstra races to give mobiles speedy online access'. *The Australian Financial Review*, 7 March, 38.

Monnier, Philippe (2001) 'Wireless information: the Japanese experience'. In *Innovations in Newspapers 2001 world report*, 52–57.

Mulligan, Christy (2001) 'Dialing for content'. *Boston Computer User*, April, 21–22.

Oksman, Virpi (2000) 'Second generation mobile media and newspapers'. Found online at http://www.uta.fi/jourtutkimus/mobiili/tiivis.htm.

Outing Steve (2000) 'Online news advice for 2001'. Found online on 27 December 2000 at http://www.editorandpublisher.com/ephome/news/newshtm/stop/st122700.htm.

Ries, Ivor (2000) 'DoCoMo's 3G mobile mission'. *The Australian Financial Review*, 25 November, 25.

Shipside, Steve (2001) '*Business a.m.* takes advantage of starting from scratch'. In PANPA *Bulletin*, June 2001.

Sinclair, Jenny (2001) 'DoCoMo goes for wireless growth'. *The Age*, 15 May, IT1.

Woo, Andy (2001) 'Wireless-led recovery'. *The Australian*, 29 May, 40.

# 7 How to involve and evolve the newsroom

## Executive summary

This chapter explores how the newsroom could evolve into a place where knowledge management flourishes. But it looks first at the dangers that rapid news cycles generate, and suggests ways to ensure that news organizations continue to produce quality journalism despite increased speed to market. It then repeats and elaborates on the need for organizations to invest in people through training and education. Much of this book has been based on the notion that leadership is needed to transform news organizations. That is, it urges that change must come from the top. But change will also come from new recruits who are comfortable with digital technology and appreciate its potential. Journalism education programmes are key to supplying these new recruits, so part of the chapter looks at the ramifications for journalism education. The chapter then provides a case study of an emerging news organization that has embraced knowledge management, the *Maeil Business Newspaper*, a daily in Seoul, Korea. The book ends with a suggested process for putting knowledge management into practice. Topics covered in this chapter include:

- ❑ danger: speed can trap the unwary
- ❑ vital to invest in training
- ❑ universities' role in the future
- ❑ the ideal journalism recruit
- ❑ a knowledge-based daily: *Maeil Business Newspaper*
- ❑ putting it all together.

The editor of *The Australian Financial Review*, Colleen Ryan, fears that reporters are becoming so 'time poor' that they cannot find what the real stories are – or check whether they are accurate. Ryan told a seminar on media in Melbourne in March 2000 that accuracy must not be allowed to suffer because of the demands of a world without deadlines. 'If we can overcome these problems – and quality publishers will – we have a truly challenging century ahead, where we can live through history with maximum information,' Ryan said. Television journalist Paul Barry, at the time the presenter of a highly respected programme on the media, told the same seminar the future of journalism would be about 'not having the time'. 'We'll be so busy filing for our 24-hour news, or our online sites, or getting the bi-media version of our stories, that we won't have time to find out what the real stories are and to check whether or not we've got them right.' Barry warned of the dangers of people saving time by going to the same sources. 'Journalists get it [stories] from wire services or the TV equivalent – a Reuters or an AP camera team whose pictures are used by everyone. Or they get it by asking other journalists. So everybody tells the same story, either because they've got it from the same source – generally an official source, a politician or a PR man – or because they've got it from each other. No one has the time to find the real stories.' Journalists needed time to reveal corruption or corporate fraud or organized crime. Media exposés of these types of things took weeks and they needed people who had built up expertise in the past, Barry said (Anonymous, 2000: 52).

## Danger: speed can trap the unwary

A combination of sophisticated newsgathering tools and information overload can mean danger for news organizations. In the dynamic world of the 24-hour news cycle, technology such as the mobile telephone, email and the Internet allow reporters to contact people quickly and obtain reaction to developing stories, and then get reaction to those reactions. Opportunities for reflection are rare. Increased speed increases the potential for errors. It becomes easier for spin doctors and other professional manipulators to deliver misinformation, especially in a business environment. Information overload can also produce errors, in the sense that journalists can misreport events because they have insufficient facts, disguised as excess data. Journalists in the information age need a heightened respect for ethics plus the ability to think clearly under pressure. These form a strong foundation from which to adapt to rapid change. Think of them as a moral compass for the information age. Another skill is the ability to learn how to learn. People spend thousands of hours getting an education, but how many hours do they spend learning how to learn? This involves skills such as knowing what is the best environment for learning, how to study properly, how to take notes effectively, how to remember large amounts of data and how to manage those data. The author of *Use Your Head*, Tony Buzan, says that all humans receive a wondrous computer at birth – but where is the manual that shows them how to use it (1989: 33)? Journalists in the digital world need another new skill: data management. Professor Tom Johnson of Boston University's Institute for Analytical Journalism has suggested that good journalists need to move past the simplistic formula of an idea plus rudimentary research to produce an adequate story. A more evolved approach, which he called the RRAWP process, is needed (1994: 58–59). The process is discussed in more detail later in the section 'Universities' role in the future'.

## Vital to invest in training

In 2000 Morgens Schmidt, then director of the European Journalism Centre, concluded in a report commissioned by the Dutch Ministry for Education, Culture and Science that the further training of journalists had become 'a permanent need'. 'Today's media are changing and developing at a pace that can only be matched through well-structured continuous training' (quoted in Bierhoff, 2000: 5). The report noted that media organizations and journalism schools had generally given priority to skill-based training ahead of knowledge-based learning. That traditional model was 'under threat'. The report suggested consideration of a new model that offered an academic education (knowledge) as a base, with the practical component (skills) introduced near the end. Regular and integrated training should be offered once people found jobs (quoted in Bierhoff, 2000: 12). Elsewhere, the news editor of the *Houston Chronicle*, Hank Glamann, advised news managers looking at introducing new systems to remember the importance of training: 'Once you've decided to move forward with a technological change, consider its impact on your newsroom work processes'. Remember, he said, that no employee could perform at their best unless they were given the tools to do the job right. Newsroom managers tended to think of tools in terms of computers on desks and related software. The most important tool editors could give journalists was knowledge. 'Our failure to provide adequate knowledge is the fundamental cause of cost of our "technological" problems. We simply do not train our people thoroughly enough to give them mastery over their machines. Is it costly, time-consuming and disruptive to provide extensive training? Yes. Does it pay off in the long run? Absolutely' (Glamann, 2000: 48).

Howard Tyner, former editor of the *Chicago Tribune* and later vice president of the Tribune company's newspaper division, said it was vital to maintain the 'journalistic soul' of the newspaper business rather than becoming obsessed with technology. His company was aiming to develop each reporter's capacity to gather content across a variety of media while ensuring that the newspaper remained at the heart of the process and quality was not diminished (quoted in Giner, 2001: 33). Tyner provided an outline in Ifra's *newspaper techniques* of how the Tribune company was working with its newspaper staff to help them learn television and radio techniques. 'Don't just throw people on the air. Work with the newspaper staff to make them comfortable on air. Determine which format is best for the content and the newspaper reporter – live interview, taped interview, pre-taped package or using the subject editor instead of the reporter. Or, just use the information and credit it to the *Tribune.*' Tyner said it was vital to provide professional coaching for newspaper reporters on how to improve their on-air presentation (quoted in Veseling, 2000: 18). Ifra's Kerry Northrup concluded that to be effective in handling cross-media news, reporters needed training in understanding which media were most effective for which aspects of a story. 'They may also be expected to take a much more active role in managing news coverage from the scene, rather than passing all the decisions to newsroom-bound editors.' News organizations needed editors who could 'think in multiple media' and who could see the story as a combination of various content elements to create an 'integrated whole'. Again, training was vital, he said, but more significantly editors needed a mindset freed from any one medium. 'A true multiple-media editor will be one who recognizes, for instance, that breaking news reporting is no longer a staple of printed journalism, and therefore that printed newspaper content must rise to a higher level while working in concert with its online siblings' (Northrup, 2000: 33). Recruiting better educated people is one way to produce higher-level content.

## Universities' role in the future

What should universities do to prepare students for future forms of journalism? Northrup described journalism education as having a 'chicken and an egg relationship' with the industry. 'Do you train journalism students for the jobs that exist today so that when they graduate they can be employed? Or do you train people for the skills that they're going to need in the news organization tomorrow so that when the newspapers come along and say "we need a new generation of journalists" they have people to pick from?' Newspapers often did not help the situation because they criticized universities for not giving journalists the skills they needed to work in the newsroom. Industry similarly criticized institutions for not training the new generation of journalists. One of the first places to start, Northrup said, was to try to make sure that journalists received training and appreciation for the strengths, weaknesses and interactions of all the different ways in which news could be disseminated. 'Most journalism programmes have been set up so that students focus just on print. I think that someone coming out of journalism school needs to have a wider understanding. Even if their specialty is in writing and not Web design, they've got to have an understanding of the strengths and weaknesses of a particular medium. So that when they approach a story they can approach it on a cross-media basis.' Northrup said it was vital students understood that a story could be told in a multiple-media form. 'So I'd say dump the print specific and get much more cross media [at university journalism programmes].' Students should be given a high level of technical expertise: 'I'm not talking about training them how to use Microsoft Access [a database program], but I am talking about training them in how to understand information management, so that when technology evolves they have the basics to understand where it's evolving' (personal interview, Melbourne, 23 July 2000).

Professor Tom Johnson has developed a formidable process for information management. The variables could be generalized as Research, Reporting, Analysis, Writing and Packaging, or RRAWP. The process involves, ideally, eight definable steps for the reporter/writer. Step one, getting an idea, is followed by the quick, initial – sometimes intuitive – formation of questions and key words related to the idea. The next step involves initial research, which leads to the formulation of new questions – the fourth step. 'Ideally, these questions, or hypotheses, expand upon former approaches to the topic and challenge old or current assumptions.' The fifth step, the gathering of data and information, is the real reporting stage. 'In the traditional application of the process, a reporter spent most of his or her time interviewing sources on the telephone or in face-to-face conversations. Today, however, an equal amount of time should be spent acquiring quantitative and textual data relevant to the issue.' The sixth step involves analysis of the collected data and information, followed by the reporter sketching an outline for the story. The eighth stage is writing the story and sending it to an editor (Johnson, 1994: 59). Professor Johnson said reporters too often took the simplistic questions of step two and jumped to step five 'with little more background than the clips from last week's issues of their own newspaper'. The resulting stories produced a level of understanding, context and perception equal to what was in 'a single year's phone book'. The key stage, Professor Johnson said, was the research. 'That means reporters go not only to the publication's or station's library for background data. They must be trained to throw a wide loop around their information resources when asking: what are the major issues relevant to a topic? What is the social, political and economic context? What is the chronology of events leading up to the current news value? Who are the most interesting and knowledgeable sources and where are they? If there is a problem, what have other locales, agencies or individuals done to solve it? What is the cliché interpretation of the topic and what seems to be leading-edge thinking and analysis? Most importantly, what seems to have gone unreported about the topic? We are, after all, in the news business' (Johnson, 1994: 59). Professor Johnson maintains that students must receive a solid grounding in fundamental library research techniques early in their degree. They should be able to transfer those generic skills to the digital environment. 'Instruction in how a library is organized and works – in tandem with training in relevant computer skills – should begin in the student's first semester at the university and/or in the journalism major. The instruction should continue and be integrated throughout the journalism curriculum at an ever-increasing level of expectation' (1994: 60).

Another perceptive journalism academic, Professor Jay Black of the University of South Florida, predicted that when students graduated they would be working in careers 'not yet imagined, employing skills and technology not yet invented' (1997). Dr Black, who holds the Poynter–Jamison endowed chair in media ethics and press policy, said that many of the jobs now available in journalism and related media did not exist a generation ago. Indeed, some did not exist a decade ago – in mid-2001 we find advertisements for positions such as content editor, information architect and multi-media producer. Dr Edward De Bono, the internationally recognized thinker, suggested that entirely new professions that involved filtering information would emerge in the coming decade: 'In the future there will emerge a series of intermediary professions – sorters, digesters, researchers – that will act as a kind of reduction valve. It is no longer possible for every user to sort through all of the information they want' (De Bono, 1999: 58). The executive director of the Center for New Media at Columbia University's Graduate School of Journalism, Professor John Pavlik, maintains that most American journalism programmes rested on late-nineteenth-century teaching models. Their curricula were organized 'along early twentieth-century technological lines'. Professor Pavlik called for the introduction of new, integrated curricula in which students were taught the principles, practices, values and standards of news reporting that cut across all media boundaries. 'Rather than learning to be "newspaper", "magazine", "television", "radio" or "online" reporters, they should simply be taught to be journalists working in a digital age' (Pavlik, 1998 and 1999).

Another talent that will be needed in the digital age is the ability to adapt in a fast-changing environment. Can this be taught? Yes, but it is better that it be learned. That is, students should take responsibility for their learning. Educators need to establish an environment in which students experience rapid change. Over time, students acquire tolerance and acceptance. But it takes time. One of the key differences between education and training is the time needed to develop the former. The Latin root for education is *educere*, as in to draw out or develop. Education is a process, during which students have qualities brought out in them, the way a wine matures in the bottle. The three or more years that people spend at university gives them time to develop. Dr Ari Heinonen of the Journalism Research and Development Centre at the University of Tampere in Finland agrees with the need to train journalists in the use of new information gathering tools. The skills required to find information on the Internet should be an essential part of the journalist's professionalism. The challenge for journalism education institutions was not to arrange Internet courses, but to make them an integral part of journalism training as a whole. 'Specialized Internet courses give exactly the wrong impression, presenting the Internet as a peculiar phenomenon instead of one natural strategy of journalistic information gathering.' It might be necessary to organize Internet training for journalists who entered the profession before it arrived and who did not have basic Internet literacy. But most journalism students were familiar with the Internet. 'In their case the training should not be limited to teaching search techniques, but future journalists should be provided with intellectual tools for processing, evaluating and contextualizing information.'

Dr Heinonen noted that the difficult part of trying to train journalists for the information age was not teaching them about technology, but showing them how to use technology in a 'journalistically purposeful way'. Many of the young people coming from school actually taught the teachers how to make the best use of the Internet. 'What is most important is how to use new technology in a journalistically purposeful way in information gathering, in building an interactive relationship with the audience, in finding new ways of presenting journalistic material – in a word: how to make new technology the servant of high quality journalism' (Heinonen, 1999).

Writer David Shenk argues that journalists are more necessary than ever in an information-glutted world. Journalists had been constructing a 'quilt of community understanding' since the dawn of civilization, disseminating new information. In a world of information scarcity, the messenger-journalist performed the vital community service of 'acquiring and transmitting fresh data'. But as information had become superabundant over the past 50 years, this hunter-gatherer role had been rendered partially obsolete. 'In a world with vastly more information than it can process, journalists are the most important processors we have. They help us filter information without spinning it in the direction of one company or another. Further, as society becomes splintered, it is journalists who provide the vital social glue to keep us at least partly intact as a common unit' (Shenk, 1997: 166–67). Shenk said the major challenge journalists faced was their willingness to share information, to manage it thoughtfully and to transform it into knowledge inside billions of individual brains. 'This is not so much fact hunting as it is data gardening.' But journalists were 'stubbornly refusing' to adapt to this new paradigm, Shenk said. The 'paramount challenge' for the modern journalist was to become 'tenders of electronic archives of all human knowledge, more like pro-active electronic librarians' than people who chased breaking news. Newsrooms needed a 'restructured value system' in which sharing and summarizing existing information became more of a priority than looking for new data (1997: 169–70). Shenk was talking about knowledge management before most people in newsrooms had even heard of the term.

## The ideal journalism recruit

What skills do employers seek when hiring journalism graduates? Ifra commissioned the Research Center at the College of Journalism and Mass Communications at the University of South Carolina to conduct a worldwide industry survey to assess the current state of video in print. Along the way the survey asked what skills editors wanted of new hires. The centre's director, Dr Lynn Zoch, said the ability to communicate in writing – such as adapting print news style to a multiple media format – was still considered more important than any visual communication skill or the ability to work in teams. Half of the respondents involved in audio or video newsgathering were still hiring people with traditional print journalism backgrounds. Three in four respondents required no special training for audio or video reporting. 'In fact, the newspapers' reporting staffs are still seen by management as primarily print reporters who adapt their work for multiple media.' But respondents indicated they wanted a different person for the multiple-media environment. Of all respondents, 65 per cent wanted to hire someone with an education in what Zoch termed 'new media journalism'. Editors for a multiple-media environment would be hired with more thought to their experience and training than were reporters, Zoch said. Four in five respondents said they hired editors with prior experience or training in multiple-media for multiple-media editing positions (Zoch, 2001).

In an article for *American Journalism Review* on the ideal journalism recruit, Cynthia Gorney said the ability to write or dictate copy quickly for multiple deadlines was essential. 'Despite the demise of afternoon dailies, early-version copy is back in a big way. Online newspaper editions are now dropping radio-style deadlines on people who used to think they were going to have all afternoon to fill out the story and work some perspective into it.' Another consequence of convergence was the need for people familiar with broadcast techniques and the ability to use online research tools (Gorney, 2000). The Gorney study was nowhere near as large or scientific as Zoch's survey, and was based solely on interviews in America. Zoch said tomorrow's journalist would be a much different person compared with the traditional reporter. They would be expected to make multiple-media news judgements, flexible enough to work in newsgathering teams and trained to use all newsgathering technology. 'Thus the *raison d'être* for the Newsplex,' Zoch said. State-of-the art newsgathering technology was being built to create a 'prototypical, multiple-media newsroom'. 'We envision a long life for the Newsplex's role in kicking today's journalists into the twenty-first century' (Zoch, 2001).

In a report for *Presstime* magazine on the state of journalism education, Carolyn Terry concluded that the digital revolution had the potential to bring about *détente* in the 'sometimes chilly relations' between the newspaper industry and journalism academia. 'For years, editors have complained that journalism-school degree holders are ill-educated, inexperienced and unprepared to step into newsroom jobs. Educators, on the other hand, bemoan the lack of industry support and face increasing pressure to move their programmes away from job training and toward a more theoretical focus. Both, however, recognize that they need co-operation more than ever'. Stephen Lacy of Michigan State University's School of Journalism in East Lansing said educators were retooling their programmes to meet the industry's changing needs. 'Most of us are reacting to what's going on at newspapers' (quoted in Terry, 2000).

Chris Harvey, a former managing editor of *American Journalism Review*, noted that cross-departmental teaching teams and professional partnerships were becoming more commonplace at university journalism programmes. The change had come about because content was rapidly evolving and journalists required an understanding not only of reporting and writing skills, but also of different media and computer coding.

Harvey, who joined the University of Maryland College of Journalism in August 2000, said universities were forging liaisons to resolve practical teaching problems. She quoted Larry Pryor, director of the online programme at the University of Southern California's Annenberg School for Communication, as saying he had drafted an agreement with his university's engineering school to teach journalism students advanced programming languages such as Perl and JavaScript. 'Mastering such languages isn't essential for young journalists seeking jobs in new media, but in some cases it can give them an edge over less tech-oriented candidates', she said. Pryor had also proposed that his university's School of Fine Arts offer a class in design to journalism students. 'They've been teaching the principles of design for years. Why should we try to reinvent the wheel?' (quoted in Harvey, 2000).

# A knowledge-based daily: *Maeil Business Newspaper*

*Maeil Business Newspaper* is the main business daily in Korea. It has a circulation of 900 000. As of mid-2001 the company ran a 24-hour cable television channel, Maeil Business TV News (MBN Ch20), along with several Internet portals, weekly publications, book publishing interests, satellite television, Web-TV, radio and wireless distribution channels for news. The company's president and publisher, Dr Dae-Whan Chang, established the television company in 1993. Dr Chang said the paper's vision was to become one of the world's most prestigious 'knowledge newspapers'. He described his organization as a 'knowledge community'. The company had become involved in using knowledge for development in 1996 when Dr Chang initiated 'Vision Korea', a national campaign to transform Korea into a knowledge-based economy. The newspaper campaigned to implement that transformation. It has initiated eight Vision Korea reports and organized six national conferences, covering topics such as the learning revolution, women's education and ways to measure knowledge management. In February 1999 the company started an Internet Korea campaign, organizing Internet education for two million housewives, 100 000 senior citizens and an undisclosed number of Army personnel. It also made available a million free Internet home pages and organized ways to give used personal computers to schools. 'We are a knowledge community.' Dr Chang said knowledge management was one of the 'trends' for the near future. 'The only way to survive in the twenty-first century is by creating knowledge.'

The organization's central 'news centre' plays a key role in disseminating knowledge and information through all possible channels. The news centre chief meets the chief editor of the newspaper and the news director of the TV channels to share story ideas. *Maeil Business Newspaper* has introduced several innovations to enhance interactivity with readers. Many newspaper articles have a colour code at the end. These can be read by a PC camera that plays a linked video file on the Internet. The paper supplies subscribers with the cameras. *Maeil Business Newspaper* provides Web and email addresses in articles, to attract reader feedback. The paper also supports more than 300 public events a year and sends reporters to universities and corporations to give public lectures. The group broadcast the first digital television programme in Korea. Digital technology allows the screen to be split into four sections, permitting delivery of large amounts of extra information. The company also pioneered the use of bio-metric scanners to personalize mobile phones and computer mice. These scanners provide extra security for reporters because no-one else can use the phones or mice (Chang, 2001).

## Putting it all together

This section of the chapter suggests a process for implementing knowledge management in a newsroom. The process is intended as a suggestion and should not be read as gospel. Nor should it be implemented in a linear or sequential way. Change is a holistic process and needs to be seen that way, not as a step-by-step formula. The process described here follows the themes outlined in Chapter 2, which looked at the need for changes in mindset, physical environment and attitudes to technology. It could be summarized as:

1  an awareness campaign, based on thorough communication

2  a training programme, based around investing in people

3  application of knowledge management processes

4  establishing 'symbols' of convergence

5  introduction of technologies to enhance this process

6  follow-up to ensure that all parties are included.

## Communication is vital

Clear and consistent communication is vital when a newsroom introduces knowledge management processes. If change is to work, from the outset people need to know why change is being introduced. Professor James Gentry, dean of the William Allen White School of Journalism at the University of Kansas, said that for a change effort to be effective, affected individuals and groups 'had to understand why the change must occur'. Professor Gentry, who has a background in management as well as journalism, has advised several publications in the change management process. 'Leadership can never communicate too much in a change effort' (Gentry, 2000). Humans dislike disruptions. They need to see the reasons for change and the reasons to change. The reasons for change are drivers outlined in the first chapter – decreasing circulation yet growing populations, information overload, changes to lifestyles producing consumers with changing information needs, and the advent of technology. Editorial managers need to show journalists how these drivers will impact on their lives, and how knowledge management could make their lives easier. If anything, the drivers are getting stronger with the passage of time. Gil Thelen, executive editor of the *Tampa Tribune*, said it was important to repeat the message as part of the communication process. 'You've got to say the same thing hundreds of times in dozens of venues before it reaches all levels of the organization. About the time you're getting bored hearing yourself talk, you're just beginning to really communicate effectively' (Thelen, 2000).

The reason to change should be sold along the lines of improving each individual's professional qualifications and standing. Paul Cheung, chief editor of *Ming Pao* in Hong Kong, said his staff accepted the concept of multi-skilling because he told them it would enhance their employment prospects. Andrew Nachison of the American Press Institute said people had to understand that information was the driver behind convergence, not the delivery platform. 'That's the lesson that can be most difficult to learn: that the newspaper, television station or Web site you once thought you worked for exclusively for is no longer your priority. You are no longer exclusive to any platform. Your priority is getting the information out on whatever platform it should be on.' Helping people accept this 'new world view' took time, training, executive leadership and money (Nachison, 2001).

Communication is especially vital in the early stages. How can managers transmit their expectations for the future? Regular meetings with key editorial staff worked at *Ming Pao*. Chief editor Paul Cheung aimed to involve all his staff. Between June and December 1999, in preparation for the move to convergence journalism, Cheung held weekly meetings with senior editorial staff. These people in turn passed the message on to their staff. Cheung used the meetings to sell new ideas: 'I aimed to show my staff that the Net was the future and journalists needed to change their approach to cope with it'. The editor of *The Age* in Melbourne, Michael Gawenda, informed staff of the need for change via meetings and a detailed letter in which he outlined the need for change. Regular newsletters are a good way to keep people informed of developments. These could be provided in paper form or on an organization's intranet. Communication reduces uncertainty. Gloria Brown Anderson, vice president for international and editorial development at *The New York Times*, related a story to show the poor levels of communication at her organization in the early 1990s. She described it as 'at the minimal level required to get the paper out every day'. 'For example, the man in circulation who was responsible for sending the daily print order to the production department, and the man in the production department who took the number, had each been in his position for 20 years. One was on the sixth floor; the other was on the fourth. They had never met.' Anderson said it really helped to formulate a vision for the organization. A series of meetings managers held in 1992 had produced a 'keystone' – a simple statement that was fundamental to the organization's strategy. Anderson described it as a philosophy in 13 words: 'Editorial excellence and independence are essential to our profitability and profit sustains them'. Anderson said a line between the business and news sides of the paper still existed, but the bonds were stronger because agreement had been reached 'as to where we can appropriately approach the line and where we cannot'. As the process of co-operation extended through the company, managers hammered out – in another 13 words – the company's core purpose: 'To enhance society by creating, collecting and distributing high-quality news, information and entertainment'. Anderson said these guiding statements had enabled *The New York Times* to pursue its goals and objectives in a more coherent and speedy fashion. The paper's strategy had three keystones: the first involved how to attract new readers; the second considered how the news side and business side could work co-operatively together; the third was how to present *Times* journalism to its audience. This involved a new awareness that the organization must, as chairman Arthur Sulzberger Jr put it, 'be agnostic about the means of delivery, be it ink-on-paper, television, radio, beepers, cell phones, portable data assistants or other media yet to be invented'. Anderson said challenges of competition, media mergers, co-opertition, the Internet, social change and the economy would continue to test her publication and all newspapers. But a commitment to editorial excellence and independence had put the paper's editors at the 'heart' of the newspaper operation. Those editors were challenged to create journalism that would accomplish the goal of 'best enhancing society'. All stages of the communication process had to 'emphasize the primacy of the editorial content' (Anderson, 2001).

## Invest in training

Talk, as the cliché goes, is cheap. So while it is important to formulate a sense of direction, money needs to be invested in training staff. If unique and compelling content is what makes a newspaper great, then money must be spent to generate that content. A related step here is the need for a marketing campaign to get consumers to know how important newspapers are to the social fabric of a society. Newspapers lead the news agenda, and the broadcast media follow up. But how many members of the public know this? The journalism profession needs to spend time and money informing the public about what they do. News organizations must also spend much more money educating their staff. Despite limited natural resources and a small population, countries like Singapore and the Scandinavian nations have managed to become world leaders through investing in knowledge. These countries spend more of their GDP on education than most other nations. In Singapore's case it is 20 per cent, the highest in the world. Sweden allocates 6.8 per cent of public spending, well above the OECD average of 5.1 per cent. On a micro level, news organizations must be willing to spend money on training and educating their staff. Traditionally some publishers have been wary of doing so, fearing that competitors will lure away their better-educated people. But journalists are more likely to stay in a stimulating environment. It is the responsibility of newsroom managers to strive to keep good people and to provide that environment.

Newspapers must also strive to attract educated staff. In 2001, almost no Australian or New Zealand news organization employed a full-time journalist with a PhD. Yet some of the world's best news organizations have recruited people with doctorates among their specialists. In continental Europe journalism is perceived as an attractive and important profession. The newspapers attract educated people. One in five of the reporters on the *Frankfurter Allgemeine Zeitung* has a PhD. The *Maeil Business Newspaper* in South Korea similarly seeks specialists to write about key subjects. Half of its journalists have at least a masters degree and 20 of its 400 editorial staff have doctorates. The paper started its own Knowledge Management Academy and offers an MBA programme in conjunction with Ann Arbor University in Michigan in the USA. Reporters are encouraged to give public lectures on their area of specialization at universities and corporations. Education is appreciated and rewarded.

The earlier section of this chapter shows that *Maeil Business Newspaper* has developed an environment that fosters knowledge management. It sponsors journalists to study abroad. The paper has its own digital campus to train IT staff, and the paper uses its newspapers in education section to teach economics to school children. Publisher Dr Dae-whan Chang said many people thought economics was difficult to learn. 'We want to change that.' Chang is the executive chairman of the World Knowledge Forum that meets in Seoul each October. 'The only way to survive in the twenty-first century is by creating knowledge, especially in a country like South Korea with its 45 million people and few natural resources, and with another 25 million poor North Koreans as neighbors' (Chang, 2001).

All news organizations should teach journalists how to manage data. All reporters should be compelled to attend basic data management courses such as how to use email filters and search engines, and how to get the best out of the company's archives. This does not need to be expensive. Most large newspapers employ people with expertise in a vast range of areas. These people can be encouraged to run courses in their specialist field for the paper's staff. A simple gesture such as a bottle of wine or a meal voucher is often more than enough payment. Many reporters will be flattered to be asked. George Landau, president of the NewsEngin company, believes knowledge management in a newsroom needs to start with tools that allow each journalist to manage his or her own information. 'Only then can this information be shared in order to give the newsroom a collective intelligence.' To reach a situation where information was shared, he said, every reporter needed to be convinced that it was in their self-interest. 'We need to get them thinking along the lines of "I wonder what useful tidbits I can steal from my colleagues today?" rather than "Why should I share all my stuff with everyone else?"' (email communication, 22 June 2001).

# Instigate knowledge management processes

Foster collaboration among staff. Appoint a knowledge management specialist and give them an office near the centre of the newsroom. Assign people to work in teams and elicit feedback from them on what worked and what did not. Show examples of successful team efforts. Highlight the achievements of prize-winning journalists who collaborated. The Pulitzer Prizes for investigative journalism offer good examples, and can be found at the Pulitzer Web site (http://www.pulitzer.org). One way to encourage collaboration is to set up environments where people can mix and mingle. The *Maeil Business Newspaper* opened a fitness club. Dr Chang said journalists often came to work early to spend time in the club and to socialize with colleagues. He found that they were more likely to spend time together discussing work. 'Often journalists come to work early to talk about a project they are working on.' Architect Saf Fahim recommends open plan areas where staff can relax and socialize. Again, they are more likely to form groups to take on projects. Integrating staff from different backgrounds was another way to establish an environment in which collaboration might evolve. When the *Orlando Sentinel* decided to move into convergence journalism its then-editor, John Haile, hired seven television journalists to work in the newsroom, with the intention that staff would learn from their colleagues. The paper also established six staff-led project teams to work on the key areas of content, work flow, technology needs and training (quoted in Gentry, 1999: 6). *Ming Pao* similarly hired experienced television reporters and based them in the paper's newsroom, so that print reporters learning convergence journalism had a resource close at hand.

# Give people a chance to play

Haile also supplied all photographers with video cameras as well as digital still cameras. Many journalists were given extensive training in on-air presentation. CNN Asia–Pacific's

John Beeston encouraged his staff to learn how to use new digital technology by playing with it: 'We gave them the gear to take home. It's the best way to learn. It takes the fear away'. CNN's senior cameramen taught reporters how to compose images in the viewfinder. 'We teach them the principles of photojournalism and editing, and then we let them play.' All 40 of the reporters on *Ming Pao*'s local desk have been working as multiple journalists since December 2000. They carry Sony digital video cameras, which range in cost from HK$12 000 to HK$20 000 (about US$1500 to US$2500). The paper's assistant editor-in-chief for multimedia news, Martin Lee, said many print journalists in Hong Kong were scared of television at first. 'Mostly it was because they knew nothing about the technology.' But once they had had a chance to play with the tools, and see how relatively easy they were to use, most did not look back, he said (personal interview, Hong Kong, 7 June 2001). All editorial staff at the Sydney headquarters of Australian Associated Press (AAP), the news agency, were given a personalized Sony mini-disk digital recorder in 2000. Editor-in-chief Tony Vermeer said they were invited to take them home to play with them. 'Play is the best way for people to lose their fear of technology' (Vermeer, 2000).

## Avoid duplication

Help people to avoid unnecessary duplication and waste of data. George Landau noted that reporters gathered vast amounts of material to tell a story but when they had finished, news organizations only kept what they published. Some organizations encouraged – sometimes even ordered – reporters to discard the supporting interviews, documents and email. 'Plenty of reporters try to hang onto this material, filling their file cabinets with old notepads and their hard drives with copies of drafts and interviews, but few of these reporters have an efficient way of organizing or searching this old material' (email communication, 22 June 2001). Rather than throw information away, editorial managers should require round or beat reporters to document their beat or round. Give them time to do so, rather than making it yet another task on top of their work day. The aim here is to render tacit knowledge in an explicit form. Offer templates to make this job easier. Make a point of creating rules and guidelines for specific editorial processes, so that people come to expect that tacit knowledge will be recorded. Organize a central database of commonly used contacts, and make it available via the intranet. Encourage reporters to use it, and make a senior editorial manager responsible for ensuring that it is regularly updated. Make a point of expecting all senior managers to be familiar with the latest newsgathering tools. Become familiar yourself. Make the intranet the home page on people's browsers and post updates about the intranet via email. Make it impossible to go further than these opening email messages until people have at least opened them. You can't force people to read them but if they open them they are more likely to read them. Put useful databases on the company intranet and publicize them via email and posters in the newsroom.

## Move the furniture and give incentives

Investigate ways to integrate similar groups of staff. For example, locate your online business reporters with your print business reporters, and your online sports staff with your print sports staff. Consider ways to get them to talk to each other and share ideas, such as offering prizes for the best report that tells a story in an integrated or multi-media form. Allan Burton-Jones points out that individuals who operate in a culture that does not share need incentives to do so. Andrew Nachison of API reported that from January 2001 the Sarasota *Herald-Tribune* had started to include journalists' involvement in multi-media in performance reviews. Journalists at *Ming Pao* receive yearly performance appraisals. Chief editor Paul Cheung awards annual pay rises at these meetings. Staff who showed commitment to integration received higher increases, he said. Aim to avoid having tribes or clans of similarly focused reporters sit together. Move the desks so that reporters and sub-editors work together. Instead of situations where reporters leave before sub-editors arrive, and never speak to each other, roster sub-editors to arrive earlier to work on feature copy that has been written the day before. Again, look for ways to get each group to talk to the other. Make reporters spend time on the copy editors' desk so they learn to appreciate the editors' role. Roster copy editors to work as reporters so they can understand the pressures that reporters face.

## Establish 'symbols' of convergence

Gil Thelen, executive editor of the *Tampa Tribune*, believes convergence requires measurable goals and 'mileage markers'. It also needed strong leaders who paid constant attention to their staff 'pushing, pulling, explaining, soothing feelings [and] moving on'. Another key that needs to be discussed is the benefit of visible symbols of convergence and knowledge management in the newsroom. The *Tribune* and other Florida papers have central news desks, often referred to as a 'symbol of convergence'. Other suggestions include the appointment of journalists with specific knowledge management roles, who should be based in the newsroom and given management support, and establishment of a resources room, again in the newsroom, where people can find out about knowledge management. Find ways to involve people and to make the changes relevant to reporters' needs. As Thelen says: 'Until convergence touches a person's life, they are only half listening'. One way to reach people is through large visual displays such as signs and television monitors.

## Use visual displays

For example, look for ways to display that day's news agenda. Possibilities include positioning large monitors on the walls that show the news list, including the list on the intranet and projecting the list via a form of video-conferencing. When Paul Cheung became chief editor of *Ming Pao* he arranged for the news list at the main news conferences to be projected onto a wall. The main editorial meeting at 18:30 h allocates stories to pages and section editors pitch for space and prominence. At this meeting, the news agenda (a Word file) is projected onto a large screen via a laptop. 'The projector gives everyone a clear view of the news list,' Cheung said. 'It also saves paper.' Architect Saf Fahim introduced several visual displays in his diagrams and plans for the Newsplex newsroom of the future. These display the news meeting agendas so that everyone in the newsroom has the option to contribute ideas. For his newsroom of the future, Fahim designed a giant news floor in the base of a large atrium, built around an amphitheatre. The idea is to hold news conferences in the open so everyone can contribute. Editorial staff work in teams on stories and their efforts are projected onto the newsroom wall. 'Anyone can see the day's news puzzle being pieced together' (quoted in Jackson, 2001: 12) Illustrations of Fahim's work can be seen in Figures 2.1 and 2.2.

## Introduce new tools for newsgathering

Train people in how to use the Internet for newsgathering. Make sure they know about the vast number of Web sites that offer links to people with specific expertise. Organizations such as ProfNet make their directories of experts available via a searchable database on the Web (http://www.profnet.com). Another source of experts that is searchable via Web sites is the Experts' directory (http://www.experts.com). Business Wire offers journalists access to its Media Resource Center. As with many sites on the Web, you need to register (http://www.businesswire.com) but it's free. Newswise (http://www.newswise.com) also requires reporters to register but this provides access to SciWire, MedWire, BizWire or LifeWire. YearbookNews is the online edition of *The*

*Yearbook of Experts, Authorities and Spokespersons* (http://www.yearbooknews.com). It has a search engine built into the home page. News Researcher Kitty Bennett at the *St Petersburg Times*, a prestigious daily in Florida, assembled a massive list of experts for her newsroom's intranet that she later made available for public consumption. Her Expert Directories Online (http://sunsite.unc.edu/slanews/internet/experts.html) tends, understandably, to be North American in tone but its range if formidable. George Landau's NewsEngin company markets SourceTracker, a tool for organizing a knowledge-based newsroom. All reporters get a personal SourceTracker in which they organize and index anything they gather or create – interview notes, email messages, documents and reports, Internet resources, spreadsheets and their original drafts of stories. The NewsEngin company provides users with two ways to share material: by marking an item for automatic copying to a shared database – the public copy is automatically updated if the reporter alters the original shared resource – or by allowing specific co-workers to access the item directly in the owner's SourceTracker. 'Until an item is shared in one of these two ways, it is regarded as private and made inaccessible to colleagues.' Landau pointed out that an organization's computer-system administrators could access any user's data, if deemed necessary by newsroom management, such as when a reporter resigned (email communication, 22 June 2001).

Give reporters mobile phones and teach them how to link them with their landline phones, so that reporters can be mobile even while expecting a call back. Put mobile numbers on reporters' business cards. Pay for Internet connections so reporters can access the Web at home. Invest in digital recorders such as the Sony mini-disk. Reporters can use them for collecting voice clips for the online site. Investigate making voice recognition software available as a way of converting digital voice files into text. Once files are in digital form they can be archived and used for generating story ideas in the future. Supply mobile devices such as Palm Pilots and other notebook computers for reporting. Re-visit the section on NewsGear in Chapter 5 for ideas and read about NewsGear in full in the 'How to learn more' section in the same chapter. Run training courses and 'brown bag' lunches where people can showcase or talk about their successes with the tools. Publicize these successes in the company newsletter.

Knowledge management provides a tool for journalists to work smarter in the twenty-first century. News executives and working reporters need to appreciate that success in the future will come from intangibles such as knowledge and innovation, rather than repeating old habits and familiar techniques such as cutting costs. Used properly and with appropriate levels of management support, knowledge management can produce better journalism. The key is to apply it. Knowledge management gives you the chance to create and work in an intelligent newsroom. What are you waiting for?

**Figure 7.1** The hub of the News Interactive headquarters in Sydney, Australia, showing the sophisticated cabling. Photograph Stephen Quinn

**Figure 7.2** The news desk of the print edition of *The Times* in London. Photograph Stephen Quinn

---

## How to learn more

---

1 Read Professor Tom Johnson's important 1994 article on information management and details about the Institute for Analytical Journalism (see this section in Chapter 2).

2 Consult books on lateral thinking by Edward De Bono.

3 Read Gorney's 'Superhire 2000' (Gorney, 2000) and Harvey's 'New courses for new media' (Harvey, 2000) in *American Journalism Review*.

4 Familiarize yourself with the Newsplex proposal. See the references section in Chapter 5 for details.

5 Organize a training course on how to use digital still or video cameras for yourself and colleagues. Form a discussion group to talk about your experiences and reflect on your attitude to training.

## References and further reading

Anderson, Gloria Brown (2001) Presentation to the World Editors' Forum in Hong Kong.

Anonymous (2000) 'Journalism standards pressured by advances in technology'. *newspaper techniques*, June, 52–53.

Bierhoff, Jan, Deuze, Mark and de Vreese, Claes (2000) 'Media innovation, professional debate and media training: a European analysis'. European Journalism Centre, December 2000.

Black, Jay (1997) 'Journalism educators' perplexing quest for relevance and respect'. Paper delivered to the 1997 annual conference of the Australian Journalism Education Association, 2 December 1997.

Buzan, Tony (1989) *Use Your Head*. London: BBC Books.

Chang, Dae-Whan (2001) 'Remaking a newspaper: *Maeil Business Newspaper* Case'. Presentation to World Association of Newspapers in Hong Kong, 6 June 2001.

De Bono, Edward (1999) 'Data digesters next: De Bono'. *The Australian*, 23 March, 58.

Gentry, James (1999) 'The *Orlando Sentinel*. Newspaper of the future: integrating print, television and Web'. In *Making Change*, a report for the American Society of Newspaper Editors, April 1999, 3–9. Also emails, June 2001.

Gentry, James (2000) 'Making change in a media environment'. Presentation to the American Press Institute in Washington, 8 June 2000.

Giner, Juan Antonio (2001) 'From media companies to "information engines"'. *Innovations in Newspapers: 2001 world report.* Innovation International Media Consulting Group 2001, 28–33.

Glamann, Hank (2000) 'Equipping employees for change'. *newspaper techniques*, January, 48.

Gorney, Cynthia (2000) 'Superhire 2000'. *American Journalism Review* 12 December.

Harvey, Chris (2000) 'New courses for new media'. *American Journalism Review* 19 December.

Heinonen, Ari (1999) 'Challenges and trends in journalism training'. Presentation to the Newsroom for a Digital Age seminar in Darmstadt, Germany, 8 December 1999.

Jackson, Sally (2001) 'Convergent views'. In the 'Media' section of *The Australian*, 28 June, 12–13.

Johnson, Tom (1994) 'Applied cybernetics and its implications for education for journalism'. *Australian Journalism Review*, July–December, 16 (2), 55–66.

Landau, George (1999) 'Newsroom as knowledge refinery'. Presentation to seminar on information technology in newsrooms, at Ifra in Darmstadt in Germany, December 1999.

Nachison, Andrew (2001) 'Good business or good journalism? Lessons from the bleeding edge'. A presentation to the World Editors' Forum, Hong Kong, 5 June 2001. Email communication 12 June 2001.

Northrup, Kerry (2000) 'New skill sets required for today's "multiple media" stories'. *PANPA Bulletin*, November, 32–33.

Pavlik, John (1998) Summary introduction to 'News in the digital age: what's next?' (a transcript of the seminar held at the Center for New Media in New York, 7 October 1998). Email communication 10 May 1999.

Shenk, David (1997) *Data Smog: Surviving the Information Glut.* San Francisco: Harper Edge.

Terry, Carolyn (2000) 'Grading the J schools'. *Presstime*, September 2000.

Thelen, Gil (2000) Presentation to API workshop, Washington, 8 June 2000.

Vermeer, Tony (2000) Personal Interview, Sydney, 31 January 2000.

Veseling, Brian (2000) 'Journalism training and education for a multiple-media environment'. *newspaper techniques*, February, 18–19.

Zoch, Lynn (2001) 'Video in print: preparing for a media convergent workplace'. Presentation to the World Association of Newspapers in Hong Kong, 5 June 2001.

# Index

The Ifra Centre for Advanced News Operations was established in 1997 to highlight Ifra's activities and leadership in issues related to technology and the future of editorial activities. NewsOps activities have expanded Ifra's credentials as an organisation with knowledge and insight concerning the future of news, newsrooms and news organisations.

*The future of the newsroom has already begun.*
*Let's talk about yours.*

Contact: Kerry J. Northrup • e-mail northrup@ifra.com • www.ifra.com

**ifra** *NewsOps*
Centre for Advanced News Operations

# Focal Press

## www.focalpress.com

Join Focal Press on-line

As a member you will enjoy the following benefits:

- an email bulletin with **information on new books**
- a regular **Focal Press Newsletter**:
  - o    featuring a selection of new titles
  - o    keeps you informed of **special offers, discounts and freebies**
  - o    alerts you to **Focal Press news and events** such as author signings and seminars
- complete access to **free content** and reference material on the focalpress site, such as the focalXtra articles and commentary from our authors
- a **Sneak Preview** of selected titles (sample chapters) *before* they publish
- a chance to have your say on our **discussion boards** and **review books** for other Focal readers

Focal Club Members are invited to give us feedback on our products and services.
Email: worldmarketing@focalpress.com – we want to hear your views!

Membership is **FREE**. To join, visit our website and register. If you require any further information regarding the on-line club please contact:

> Emma Hales, Marketing Manager
> Email: emma.hales@repp.co.uk
> Tel: +44 (0) 1865 314556
> Fax: +44 (0)1865 314572
> Address: Focal Press, Linacre House,
> Jordan Hill, Oxford, UK, OX2 8DP

### Catalogue

For information on all Focal Press titles, our full catalogue is available online at www.focalpress.com and all titles can be purchased here via secure online ordering, or contact us for a free printed version:

| **USA** | **Europe and rest of world** |
| --- | --- |
| Email: christine.degon@bhusa.com | Email: jo.coleman@repp.co.uk |
| Tel: +1 781 904 2607 | Tel: +44 (0)1865 314220 |

### Potential authors

If you have an idea for a book, please get in touch:

| **USA** | **Europe and rest of world** |
| --- | --- |
| editors@focalpress.com | focal.press@repp.co.uk |